SHARE JESUS FEARLESSLY

A Simple Guide to Evangelism

Donnie Anthony

WESTBOW
P R E S S®
A DIVISION OF THOMAS NELSON
& ZONDERVAN

WestBow Press books may be ordered through booksellers or by contacting:

WestBow Press
A Division of Thomas Nelson & Zondervan
1663 Liberty Drive
Bloomington, IN 47403
www.westbowpress.com
1 (866) 928-1240

ISBN: 978-1-9736-1818-8 (sc)
ISBN: 978-1-9736-1819-5 (hc)
ISBN: 978-1-9736-1817-1 (e)

Library of Congress Control Number: 2018901370

Print information available on the last page.

WestBow Press rev. date: 06/07/2019

This book is dedicated to two people who have
impacted my life immeasurably and encouraged
me to be the witness for Christ I am today.

The first is Trinetta, my wife of thirty-two years. You have
been my greatest cheerleader in the ups and downs of serving
Jesus together in ministry, and you have been my most honest
critic when I needed a swift kick in the rear. I love you forever.

The second is the legendary evangelist Lee Castro. You took
me under your wing when I was eighteen years old, and
God used you to ignite a passion for sharing Jesus as we sang
and preached in churches and prisons and bars. That flame
ignited many years ago is still burning forty years later.

I have known of Donnie's passion for evangelism for several years dating back to his time in student ministry. Donnie continuously raised up students who were intentional about engaging the culture with the gospel. However, a couple of years ago, I got the see his love for evangelism up close as I served his church as interim pastor. It was in this context that I began to see that Donnie was not just a trumpeter of evangelism; he was a practitioner as well.

I must admit, I was excited to learn that Donnie was working on a book on evangelism. In my role, I am always looking for resources to help churches in the practice of evangelism. I have learned the greatest people to write on the topic are those who do it! So it is with joy that I ask you to prayerfully consider this work as a tool to help Christians better engage their sphere of influence with the gospel.

— Nathan Lorick, executive director, Colorado Baptist General Convention, former director of evangelism, Southern Baptists of Texas Convention

When one writes out of one's passion, the rest of us are beneficiaries of the overflow of the work God has done. Donnie Anthony has been able to capture his passion on the pages of his work, which instructs, encourages, and inspires believers to join in the apostles' early witness that "we cannot stop speaking what we have seen and heard."

I have known Donnie for the past thirty-five years, and his love for both Christ and those who need Christ continues to be cultivated through a life of obediently following the simple command of Christ to share the good news.

Donnie has tested his expression of the Helping Hand to Christ in multiple cultural and global contexts with immeasurable success. His "Helping Hand to Christ" is not only easy to understand but readily reproduced in others demonstrated in multiple generations of the believers who have embraced this model. In his work *Share Jesus Fearlessly*, Donnie proves that God can transform a willing heart into an effective witness for the glory of God.

—Dr. Rodney Woo, PhD, pastor, International Baptist Church, Singapore

I'm writing to recommend my friend and co-laborer's book, *Share Jesus Fearlessly*, for your consideration. Over these past years, I have seen Donnie live and teach these principles to hundreds of people. He lives and breathes evangelism and is effective in not only teaching others but in communicating in such a way that others become passionate about the gospel.

In this book, Donnie effectively shares his story as well as how others can share God's story. Donnie's methods are clear and concise and communicate in a way that everyone can understand and apply.

I would highly recommend this book and see in it a huge kingdom benefit.

—Matt Surber, lead pastor, Castle Hills Church

ACKNOWLEDGMENTS

Don and Marie Anthony—Mom, you instilled in me from my earliest years a love for Jesus. Dad, you taught me the Roman Road to Salvation when I was still a child. Your example of loving people and leading them to Jesus was the first spark that God used to ignite my passion for evangelism.

Rodney Woo—my friend, my brother, my mentor. Your counsel has guided me through rocky waters and encouraged me to press on.

Bob and Sharon Bayless—thank you for being constant supporters and key players in the development of The Helping Hand to Christ. For many years you have poured countless hours into training people to share Jesus and inspired me to keep on keeping on.

Lee and Brenda Gallegos—you were there in the very beginning of this work. And you have been such faithful ministry partners and friends.

Rick Elizondo—my prayer and accountability partner for over fourteen years! This book would never have been published without your support.

Raymond Gibson—you were there when I had almost given up on getting this in print. Nobody inspires me more to think big and expect God to do amazing things. Thanks.

Marcia Voigt, Colleen Davis, and Cherie George—each of you said to me that you hoped you were not too brutal in the editing process. You are angels who rescued me from the pit of bad punctuation.

INTRODUCTION

Heart Attack at Age Eighteen!

A heart attack at eighteen! Well, kinda. It was the fall of 1975, and I found myself sitting in a church in the hills of Kentucky listening to a fundamentalist Baptist preacher. I was eighteen years old and had left home three days after graduating from high school to travel as a musician doing Christian concerts and revivals. It was my dream. All I wanted to do was play music, and my ship had come in. I loved it. On this night, though, I was a little fatigued from the grind of being on the road and was not really plugged into the message. That was until the speaker suddenly said something that fell on me like a window washer whose scaffold had come unlatched ten stories up. It was my first time to hear this startling statistic: "Ninety-five percent of all Christians will live and die and never know what it's like to sit down with someone and tell them how to miss hell and make heaven." In that moment, sitting on that oak pew in Kentucky, I suddenly saw myself standing before God empty-handed. In an instant, the thought of standing before God having done little to nothing to personally point someone to Christ became unthinkable. How could I live and die hoarding truth that would leave someone's soul hanging in the balance? It would be inexcusable. I felt God mounting an all-out assault on the hard shell that had formed over my heart, and the attack was more than I could withstand. I have only experienced the blessing of this level of brokenness a few times in my life. Like one of those shiny kitchen hammers my mom used to use to tenderize meat, God had pulverized my heart, and the words from the pages of Ezekiel became real to me that day: "I will remove the heart of stone from your flesh and give you a heart of flesh." No one wakes up one day and decides to be broken. It is a gift from our sovereign God. I have been thankful every day, for that gift which was delivered directly to my heart on that evening.

Through this gift of brokenness, God has taught me to grieve over those who do not yet know Him. That night catapulted me into the most exhilarating adventure of my life, which I have come to call "the evangel adventure." I invite you to come along on that adventure. I hope this book will help you take steps that will allow you to easily engage people in a way that will help them consider the claims of Christ without being offensive or pushy.

My heart is still broken to this day. It's broken for the lost still, but there is another kind of brokenness that has settled into my heart as well. It is a brokenness for those who know Christ but have never been able to lead another person to a place where they can say yes or no to Jesus. This has become my life passion. You know when you discover your life passion because you clearly see a condition in this world that so grieves you that you are willing to invest your life to change it. It's been forty years since that night in that rural church. And this small body of work is the least I felt I could do make a dent in this sad condition of believers who do not feel like they can confidently share the gospel. I assure you that this will not turn into a guilt trip but an open invitation for people to join the noble adventure of sharing the good news of Jesus Christ fearlessly. This does not mean that you will never again feel that twinge of nerves as you begin to talk about Jesus. It just means fear will not paralyze you into inaction.

Why do I start here? Because, you can have all the biblical knowledge in the world crammed into your head, but if that amazing high-performance brain isn't coupled with a heart broken for others, we become a clanging cymbal. "If I speak in the tongues of men or of angels, but do not have love, I am only a resounding gong or a clanging cymbal" (1 Corinthians 13:1). We can know and speak Bible truth until we are blue in the face, but if we are not sharing out of a broken heart that truly loves, it sounds a lot like a six-year-old with his first drum set on Christmas morning. People don't care how much you know until they know how much you care.

It does all begin with a broken heart. Would you dare to ask God for one? I stated earlier that no one just decides to get broken; it's a gift from God. But I also know that God wants you to have this broken heart because it aligns your heart with His.

I hope you will journey with me through this book. It's my intention to not only give you practical tools to know how to share Christ but along the way to hopefully instill this broken heart that's so essential.

So What's the Problem?

I love the family of God. I love how I have experienced such love and empathy and forgiveness and mercy and all-out crazy good times with them. And as I have done life together with so many followers of Jesus, it's become evident to me that the ones who really do love Jesus also really love people. And it goes without saying that they honestly can't bear the thought of any person spending eternity apart from God in a place called hell. So, here's my question: If so many followers of Jesus love Him and care about the lost, then why aren't more of us sharing the good news of Jesus Christ?

It's because something is missing from the equation. In fact, there are several things missing from the equation. Please don't stop reading here. I understand this noble mission of bringing the lost to saving faith cannot be reduced to a math problem. But there is a holy equation that represents God's heart. Here is that equation: passionate followers of Christ + brokenness for those without Jesus + a simple way to share Jesus = an evangelism revolution.

If we are going to see the gospel move out in wave after wave swelling to a tsunami in the body of Christ, we've got to bring these factors together.

It's my hope that this book, which has taken several decades to live out and then write down, will spur you onward and upward in each of these areas. I believe with all my heart it can happen to you. It can happen in you.

Why do I believe this? For two reasons. First, because I have personally experienced it. I have seen God lift me out of the pit of apathy and mediocrity to a place where I get up every morning wondering who I will intersect with that day and how God will impact their lives.

The second reason is because I have been so blessed to spend the last nine years of my life training people in personal evangelism in the laboratory of the local church. I've seen all types of people go from having a timid spirit to becoming bold witnesses. These average church members have become passionate lovers of Christ, have had their hearts truly broken for those who have not yet trusted Christ, and they've learned a simple way to share Jesus. The result is that a spirit of fear has been transformed into one of power, love, and a sound mind.

Perhaps a few stories will help.

Keary is a high-powered wealth advisor. He's one of the most confident guys you will ever meet. He's truly a captain of enterprise, but that confidence did not extend into the area of sharing Jesus. He shared with me that he simply lacked a plan. He came to our training and took off like a rocket. On several occasions, he would call me in the middle of his workday to ask me to pray because he was about to share Jesus with a salesman or a colleague.

Edika grew up as a pastor's kid and knew the Bible better than most. She had taught Bible studies for years, had led women's retreats for her denomination and was even the executive assistant to the head of a theological seminary but wasn't sure how to confidently share her faith. Edika finally learned the why and the how of sharing Christ, and now she has had the privilege of seeing many come to know Christ. She has found the joy of knowing how to get started in talking about the gospel, and more importantly, how to draw the net when fishing for men.

Bob and Sharon are a couple who trained with us years ago and have gone on to not only train many but to teach the class on how to share Jesus. Sharon has taught women to share Jesus at retreats as well. Their testimony is that learning to share Jesus has enriched their marriage.

One of my favorites is Lee, a man who became broken for the lost and saw it transform him spiritually. He shares Jesus regularly and has gone on to train people who in turn have trained others to share Jesus confidently in any situation. Lee is very aware that he has a part in every person any of them may get to lead to saving faith in Jesus.

Harold is a senior adult who had a desire to be more prepared to share Jesus. He came to learn how to share Jesus using the Helping Hand to Christ but was self-conscious because his hand had been ravaged by severe arthritis. With a little encouragement, he learned this powerful approach and had the opportunity to use it to lead his own brother to Christ just months before he passed away.

Ken was also a senior adult who had a passion to share Christ with his large extended family, including his children and grandchildren. He came and learned how to share Jesus and was eventually able to share the gospel with his entire extended family at their annual Thanksgiving meal.

And finally, there is Stan. Stan is a friend of mine with special needs. He heard about our witness training from Lee. For several years Lee picked him up and brought him, and he learned how to share Jesus. Through patience and repetition, Stan learned how to present the gospel, and suddenly, he became a witness for Christ who was on fire. Every week at our prayer time, Stan would share the names and stories of those with whom he had shared that week. In simple, slow terms he talked about leading people to Jesus on the city bus, at the bus stop, and at the store where he worked. He was a constant reminder that anyone can share Jesus.

CHAPTER 1

The First Time

So there I was, my heart broken for the lost, determined to leave the paralysis of spiritual inactivity to do something for God. I've always felt like I could do anything I set my mind to, so I set out to "save somebody." Surely, as we traveled across the country, I would be able to tell some cashier at a gas stop about Jesus. Surely, I would meet someone who would practically run up and ask me, "What must I do to have eternal life?" But nothing happened.

Then God, as He often does with His kids, put me in an interesting position. I ended up with a rare week off and returned to my hometown, Corpus Christi, Texas, for a visit. When you are eighteen years old and back in your hometown the fall after graduating from high school, it's natural to visit a favorite coach or teacher and make fun of the poor, pitiful souls still enduring the public school system. So I did. I went back to Roy Miller High School, determined to visit the only teacher/coach I knew who would let me disturb his class: my old tennis coach, Coach Peebles.

The year was 1975, but the memory of what happened next is vivid. I was walking up the stairs at the school and ran into Eddie. Even though he was a year behind me, we had shared a few classes. I greeted him and asked the obligatory, "How have you been?"

His answer startled me a little. "Terrible."

I had asked a nonquestion while expecting to get a nonanswer, but this guy caught me off guard by being honest. Right there in the hallway, he cracked open a window into his heart.

It's a curious and almost exclusively Western Hemisphere practice to ask the same question over and over in a day without any real sincerity. We keep asking people, "How are you doing?" and they keep saying, "Fine." But many who utter the word *fine* are anything but fine. And every now and again, someone at wit's end who has had enough really tells us the truth, and we're not sure how to deal with it. I had hit Eddie on one of those days. He was in one of those seasons of life during which you just don't care anymore. It was one of those times when your quiet desperation oozes from the place you've been hiding it and leaks from your mouth in a moment of honesty.

At the same moment Eddie's desperation leaked out, the Holy Spirit reminded me of the 95 percent. So Eddie was just standing there with his huge, dominating football self. This was the first true divine appointment I recognized after having my heart broken by God, and I knew it was my time. I had to share how a life that's broken down can be broken open to the love of God that heals. It was my moment to share Jesus.

God not only has a wonderful sense of humor but also an impeccable sense of timing. You see, I was a thousand miles from home when I made the commitment to share His name, assuming (and preferring) that it would be with someone I had never met. I thought it would be a stranger, but God wanted me to share in the hardest place first: at home with those who knew me best. And that part about knowing me best? That's what made this experience awkward. You see, I had not only failed in talking about Jesus that year before in high school, but walking with God had not been a priority either. The thought of my hypocrisy was paralyzing.

I was standing there pretty much in shock as Eddie went on to say that his family was falling apart, his relationship with a girl had just ended, and he was at the point where he just didn't care about anything anymore. I knew Eddie loved cars, so I asked him if he'd like to go for a drive in the car I had recently purchased, and he agreed. While we were driving around talking more about how his life had spiraled out of control, I remember grasping for words. I had learned the verses for the Roman Road to salvation as a child, but they just weren't coming; it had been too long. I lacked the training needed for the moment, but God was faithful to give me the words to tell Eddie my story. I shared how God had given me not only the assurance of heaven someday but that He had given me peace and meaning in my life now.

I finally asked, "Would you like to have that same kind of friendship with God?" and when Eddie said yes, I almost wrecked that 1972 Thunderbird. Once again God honored His promise to give us the words to say when we find ourselves in the moment and on the spot. I told Eddie how I had prayed to receive Jesus and led him in an awkward but honest prayer of trust and commitment to Christ.

It's hard to explain what I felt when Eddie prayed, and I realized that eternity was forever changed in an instant. I had witnessed the greatest miracle of all: a changed heart that just moments before had been racing toward hell, drowning in despair, but was now not only promised the reality of heaven but was also relieved of the huge weight he'd been carrying through life. His countenance was new; it was like I was looking at someone else entirely.

Along with my own experience of salvation and my children coming to know the Lord, this experience still ranks among the most powerful spiritual moments of my life. And once you have been there in such a powerful moment in history, you yearn to experience it again. Not for experience's sake but because there was absolutely no doubt in that instant that God was speaking through you.

For those few moments, nothing else I could be doing was as important as what God was doing through me. It was the beginning of a lifetime of situations in which God would allow me to share His good news, and today I remain very aware of the deep joy God feels at the sight of one of His kids just being excited about who He is and what He can do in another person's life.

CHAPTER 2

Let It Flow—or Overflow!

Through my first attempts at sharing Christ and my encounter with Eddie, I had stumbled onto what I now know to be the real secret to sharing Jesus with others. Sharing Christ doesn't involve marching off, independent of God, to witness "for" Him. Authentic evangelism is Christ in me revealing Himself to others He loves deeply. If I had walked out of that church in Kentucky and convinced the next three people I met to pray the sinner's prayer, I might still be operating in the flesh. There are people out there who operate that way. A pastor friend told me of an incident that happened as he was leading a group through a tour of the Holy Land. During the trip, a certain lady shared with him that she had already decided on a set number of people that she would "save" before returning home. Now I realize it is within the realm of possibility that God could give a person such a number, but I knew this lady and given her "turn or burn" method of confrontational evangelism, I think we would be on safe ground to assume otherwise.

I remember being asked in a group one day what we thought

was the primary attribute of God. The consensus was that God's primary attribute surely must be love, in keeping with 1 John 4:8. But the speaker went on to share that the most basic attribute of God is that He is a revealing God. While it is true that God is love, the fact is that His love flows out of His desire for relationship. He reveals Himself to man to enter a personal relationship with him. If God were not both compassionate and revelatory in nature, He would simply sit, self-sufficiently, in heaven and enjoy His own glory. It would be enough. But because He is a revealing God who loves and deserves to be loved in return, we can share Christ with the confidence that He is making Himself known to those with whom we share this good news. This has been a revolutionary idea that has changed the way I think about sharing Jesus. I, like many believers, used to think of evangelism primarily in terms of duty. In order to appease God and comfort my own guilt, I needed to try to talk someone else into faith in Christ. This led to me thinking that I was only successful when a person dropped to his or her knees and trusted Christ on the spot. I now see that God is revealing Himself through my lifestyle and conversations. When people reject the truth, I simply see them as people whose faith is incomplete. It's a natural part of the process of God revealing Himself to the world that not everyone gets it immediately. The simple analogy that scripture uses to illustrate this is that of farming.

When I approach someone and give a clear verbal witness, I may be only clearing away stones from the field of their hearts as a farmer would on his first day of farming a new plot of ground.

When I say the truth, I may be plowing ground that has become hardened by life burdens. I might be the one to put the seed into the ground, or my role could be watering a tender plant another faithful person planted with his or her honest exchange. It could be that we find ourselves weeding in our Father's garden and at some time, if we are faithful, we will participate in the harvest of seeing a person put his or her trust in Jesus as Savior. The real point here is that none of these roles can be elevated above the other, and not one of them is of our own doing. The apostle Paul speaks clearly to this in 1 Corinthians 3:5–8: "I planted, Apollos watered, but God was causing the growth. So then neither the one who plants nor the one who waters is anything, but God who causes the growth. Now he who plants and he who waters are one; but each will receive his own reward according to his own labor" (NIV).

There is such a difference in how we share the good news of Jesus when we truly understand that we are not standing alone in the Father's fields trying hard to convince some soul of something. Instead, we get to join the Father in His fields as He reveals himself to people by having the very life of Jesus flow as living water from deep within my heart into the life of another person. In John 15:5, Jesus says, "I am the vine, you are the branches; he who abides in Me and I in him, he bears much fruit, for apart from Me you can do nothing." This statement is true in every arena of life, especially when it comes to sharing Jesus. The fruit of a believer is another believer, but we cannot produce such amazing, supernatural results. This mind-set of simply allowing God to flow through us to others keeps us from operating in the flesh.

It also frees us from the deluded thought that our effectiveness in sharing Christ is dependent on our own wisdom or the power of our personality. Some of the most effective witnesses I know do not have the gift of gab, nor do they possess charismatic personalities. They do, however, know how to be dependent on God. We are the faucet, not the water, and God is setting up divine appointments in our lives during which His Holy Spirit will turn on the faucet and allow living water to flow.

If God has not called us to simply spout scriptures to unsuspecting bystanders, if it's more than being on the God squad, assaulting people with our high-powered doctrine guns, then what is it supposed to look like? Sharing Jesus should be as natural as a father bragging on his son or a grandfather his grandchildren. I have never met a grandparent who talks about his or her grandchildren in a timid, apologetic way. I have, on the other hand, seen many a grandparent with a smartphone loaded with pictures of a grandbaby just waiting for any opportunity to show them to anyone who will listen and look. The conversations that follow are not shallow or awkward but filled with passion. One of the key passages in the New Testament that has guided me to sharing Jesus is found in 1 Peter 3:15.

> But in your hearts set apart Christ as Lord. Always be prepared to give an answer to everyone who asks you to give the reason for the hope that you have. But do this with gentleness and respect. (1 Peter 3:15 NIV)

The first phrase of this passage, "But in your hearts set apart

Christ as Lord," is where it all begins. There is nothing as annoying to me as a spokesperson on television endorsing a product that we all know he doesn't really use (or which he began using a week before the commercial aired). Endorsing "religion" is a poor substitute for sharing about my personal relationship with God. However, sharing passionately about my relationship with God presupposes that I have one! Before Peter talks about sharing the reason for the hope in us, he shares the key to effectiveness, "set apart Christ as Lord." This doesn't just mean that He becomes the boss of me. It means He becomes the joy of my life. This starts with assurance of our salvation and continues as we walk daily in the Spirit.

I will never forget being at a conference at the Billy Graham Evangelistic Retreat Center in the Blue Ridge Mountains of North Carolina. One hundred pastors from around the country had been invited to meet with some of the top Christian leaders in America. I had only gotten the invitation by default because we had lost our senior pastor and it was related to missions. I arrived to find myself riding in a shuttle up to the meeting area with the likes of Loren Cunningham, the founder of Youth With A Mission, John Piper, the author who had turned my theology upside down with *Let the Nations be Glad*, and Henry Blackaby, whose work *Experiencing God* was used by God as one of the greatest spiritual renewals I have seen in my lifetime.

When we took a break for dinner, I was so excited that God opened up a door for me to eat with Henry Blackaby, the author of *Experiencing God*, who has sold over seven million copies of that one work alone. Finally, after just listening and soaking up truth for a good while, I took this opportunity to ask him, "Why is it that ninety-five of all believers will never sit down with someone and share the gospel?" His response was quick. He didn't mull it over or scratch his chin in an academic pause; he immediately said, "It's because they do not have a love relationship with Him." He stated that he believed that the most exciting part of people's salvation story should be all the wonderful adventures they have experienced as a result of being a friend of the God of the universe. However, the reason most people only get around to talking about the circumstances through which they prayed to trust Christ as Savior is because very little has happened since that time. It is easy to talk about something that impacts your life daily. People tell me all the time about their new diet, their new car, their new workout, or the gym they have joined. Why? Why do they talk so freely about these things? Because they have made an impact on their lives that month, that week, or that very day! But many of us go through entire seasons of life when we have so little interaction with God in our daily lives, thoughts, and conversations that it's as if He is the God who "changed" me back then when I believed instead of the God who changes my life moment by moment.

The key, then, to sharing the good news of Jesus is to share out of the overflow of a life that is vitally connected to the Savior. It is so much more effective than being reduced to attempting to guilt people into the kingdom. The motive and the mode of our bearing witness to Christ will determine our delivery. People can tell the difference between those who are going door to door spreading religion because they have been goaded into it and those who want people to experience the same amazing change He has made in their lives.

When God moved our family from Houston, Texas, to San Antonio, we were excited, and one of the reasons was because of the theme parks there. At the time, our boys were nine, six, and five years of age. One of the theme parks in our area is Sea World, famous as the home of Shamu the killer whale. We quickly learned that the highlight of a day at this park was the sea lion, otter, and Shamu show. (The real attraction for adults on hot summer days in San Antonio is the chance to sit in the shade and avoid long lines.) Once you learn that this show is the must-see event of the day, you get really savvy and learn to get there early so you can get the best seats in the house: in the splash zone.

What is the splash zone? It is made up of the several rows of chairs located just in front of the tank where Shamu does his special tricks, one of which is pushing a small tidal wave across the pool until it pours over the top of the Plexiglas, drenching the lucky folks who waited thirty minutes extra to sit in the chosen seats. The crowd gets a big laugh out of the element of surprise, and frankly, the cool water can feel very refreshing on a hot summer day in Texas. (As I was reflecting on this later, my enthusiasm waned when it dawned on me that they do not let Shamu out to use the restroom!) Our family felt very special when we sat in the splash zone. It is a lot more fun to live in the splash zone when it comes to sharing our faith as well. I am reminded of what Jesus said to the crowds gathered at the Feast of Booths in Jerusalem, "If anyone is thirsty, let him come to Me and drink.

He who believes in Me, as the Scripture said, 'From his innermost being will flow rivers of living water'" (John 7:37–38 NIV). It was always God's plan that the good news of eternal life would overflow from joy deep within us. The result is that those who are in the splash zone then receive it as refreshment to their soul.

This overflowing kind of life is the result of walking moment by moment in relationship with Jesus and is what the Bible refers to as "walking in the Spirit." Conversely, the life of religious duty that tries to earn God's favor is one of the ways people "walk in the flesh." If we are walking in the Spirit, then our verbal witness to others will be in the Spirit. If we are in the flesh, our words will be fleshly as well. Since this is such an important key to sharing Christ, it is worthy of our further consideration.

How'd we get into this pattern of flesh? When we receive eternal life, what comes next? For many of us, the "what's next" was to get busy doing lots of stuff for God so He would be pleased with us and bless us. This only seems natural since our mind has been filled with this pattern since we were toddlers. We acted nicely because Mommy and Daddy love little boys and girls who are good. We performed in the classroom because our teachers loved good students. We excelled on the sports field or court because our success won us the approval of coaches and fans alike. And many of us are still on the performance treadmill at work. You might say it's natural for us to perform. But it's supernatural for us to learn to let God perform His works through us. His economy runs counter to the natural.

I was a child when I heard a pastor say, "I don't understand how a black and white cow can eat green grass and give white milk and yellow butter … but I like it." I don't fully understand where the electricity comes from that is used to illuminate my living room, but I still gladly enjoy it. Likewise, I don't understand how God could cover such a flawed clay pot as I am with the holiness and righteousness of His own perfect Son, giving me His once and for all unconditional stamp of approval. *That* is an amazing kind of grace. Now I not only have the approval of God, but according to the apostle Paul, the very life of Jesus has replaced the death that reigned in my heart. Paul says it this way: "I have been crucified with Christ; and it is no longer I who live, but Christ lives in me; and the *life* which I now live in the flesh I live by faith in the Son of God, who loved me and gave Himself up for me" (Galatians 2:20 NIV, emphasis mine).

From the moment I took my first breath, there was a death penalty hanging over me as a result of sin. Death was always present in me, methodically working its way into every area of my life. However, Jesus did more than merely remove the death sentence; He put His very own life in me. This is the key to living life in the Spirit. As I walk with God, I learn how to strip away any remaining shreds of the grave clothes that used to cover me. I cast off things such as worry, sinful habits, and even my striving to do good works apart from God. These are all simply ways that we "walk in the flesh." Some of these are roadkill flesh—deadly habits like drug addiction and sexual sin—and some of these are USDA prime beef flesh, such as doing good things for the praise of men. Even so, every act is either of flesh or of the Spirit. The dividing line between flesh and Spirit is drawn along the border of dependence and independence. If man is doing it apart from God, it is flesh. If God is accomplishing it through us, it is Spirit. The apostle Paul said in Romans 14 that whatever is not of faith is sin. Our confidence in God's ability to reveal Himself through us allows us to share Christ in the Spirit.

Galatians 5:16–18 speaks plainly of this concept when it states, "So I say, walk by the Spirit, and you will not gratify the desires of the flesh. For the flesh desires what is contrary to the Spirit, and the Spirit what is contrary to the flesh. They are in conflict with each other, so that you are not to do whatever you want. But if you are led by the Spirit, you are not under the law" (NIV). In a sense, this means that there is only one sin that all other sins fall under: acting independently of God. Jesus lived His life continually walking in the Spirit. Whether it was to a bustling city or to the desert, we read that Jesus was "led of the Spirit." Also, we never find Jesus acting independently of God. In fact, in the great temptation of our Savior by Satan himself, there was only one real temptation: to act independently of His father. Turning stones into bread when the Father had said to fast, throwing Himself onto the front steps of the temple for all to see the angels rescue Him, or bowing in worship to anyone but the Father were all really attempts to lure Jesus away from life in the Spirit. Listen carefully to His own testimony of how He lived life:

> Truly, truly I say to you, the Son can do nothing
> of Himself, unless it is something He sees the
> Father doing; for whatever the Father does, these

things the Son also does in like manner. (John
5:19 NASB)

If this really is what the great writer Watchmen Nee calls the "normal Christian life," then it revolutionizes my view of sharing the Good News of Christ with others. I don't ever have to imagine myself thrust out by God into the harvest field with a pruning hook and His best wishes to do whatever I can. In John 15 Jesus made it clear how much I can do apart from Him when He said, "But without me you can do nothing." The portrait of a faithful witness that has been etched into my mind is one of a believer being enveloped by the Holy Spirit that moves him to the next divine encounter. When I find myself at that next opportunity, all I need to do is relax, stay surrendered, and allow the life of Jesus to flow through me. Sound easy enough? Yes, it sounds easy, but for me, wrapped up in that phrase "relax and stay surrendered" is a lifelong battle to realize that I am crucified with Christ, that my identity has changed and I simply need to walk in the reality of who I am in Christ.

CHAPTER 3

You Can't Give What You Don't Have

The question of how to share Jesus is secondary to a more foundational question that we must answer. It is the beginning place not only for those who desire to impact their world but really for every person on the planet. Here is the question *you* should ask yourself: Are you 100 percent certain that if you died right now, you would go to heaven? It's very simple. If you have ever opened your life to Christ by placing your trust in Him alone for eternal life, then you have that eternal life. If not, then you do not have eternal life. This stark reality is stated in such certain terms in 1 John 5:12, "Whoever has the Son has life; whoever does not have the Son of God does not have life" (NIV).

It's amazing how many people who claim to be Christ followers have serious doubts about their security in Christ. Some who have come to me for counsel have struggled for months or even years over this question, and for many it's kept them up at night. Some have worried themselves into a debilitating depression.

A simple truth from God's word addresses this powerfully. The Bible teaches that today is the day of salvation, and *now* is the time to become sure. There is no good reason to wait. You have nothing to gain by putting this off. You can put your trust in Jesus alone at this moment!

Continuing to entertain such doubts opens the door for Satan to get his big toe in, and given time, he will move from a toehold to a foothold and eventually a stronghold. How does this relate to sharing Jesus? Well, a person swimming in doubt and fear about his or her own relationship to God will not share such a shaky faith with others.

You cannot give away that which you do not possess. Some people say things like, "I've always believed in Jesus," or "Somewhere along the way, I just believed and got saved." The easiest way to see the fallacy of this is through the analogy of marriage. Imagine someone saying, "I have always been married," or "Somewhere along the way, I just became married." Nonsense! First of all, if you are married, you are well aware of it. And second, there was a precious moment when you, in a sobering act of your will, said, "I do," and your life changed in an instant.

I love talking about my wedding. I love remembering that it was March 9, 1985. I love to remember the details of what songs were played and who stood for us and who signed our marriage license as witnesses. If you have experienced the equally life-changing event of placing your trust in Jesus for eternal life, then you should be able to recall the when and where and what of that event. When and where did that happen for you? Where were you when you put your trust in Jesus Christ alone for your eternal life? I am not asking if you walked down an aisle at a church or a summer camp service. Many a person has had a similar experience that fell short of putting their trust in Jesus. I am not asking when you said a prayer. These things can be done without a true heart change. The real question is, have you ever transferred your trust away from self and put it squarely in Jesus Christ? You see, Acts 16:31 says, "Believe in the Lord Jesus Christ and you shall be saved," and it is important that we fully understand the word *believe* in its biblical context because we use it in so many ways in our culture. We say things like, "I believe it's going to rain today." In this context, the word *believe* means "a distinct possibility." Or we may say, "I believe that there is too much government intrusion in our lives." In this context, the word *believe* is reduced to "my opinion is …" However, in the New Testament, it carries a different meaning, a different weight.

Notice some of the passages where various forms of this word *believe* occur:

> Whoever *believes* and is baptized will be saved, but whoever does not *believe* will be condemned. (Mark 16:16 NIV)

> Those along the path are the ones who hear, and then the devil comes and takes away the word from their hearts, so that they may not *believe* and be saved. (Luke 8:12 NIV)

> They replied, "*Believe* in the Lord Jesus, and you will be saved—you and your household.'" (Acts 16:31 NIV)

That if you confess with your mouth, "Jesus is Lord," and *believe* in your heart that God raised him from the dead, you will be saved. (Romans 10:9 NKJV)

In each case, the word *believe* is a form of the Greek root word *pisteuo*, and the true meaning of the word is much more than being hopeful of something or having a strong feeling about something.

The simplest and best picture I have ever heard of this word was from the late Dr. D. James Kennedy, who illustrated this for his audience by placing a single chair in the front of the room. He then asked the audience if they believed in that chair, to which they responded yes. You see, they saw the chair and trusted that it was not a hologram but a tangible object. They went even further to think in their hearts that this chair was probably a strong chair fully capable of holding their weight. "But," he explained, "you are not really trusting in this chair until you sit down." When we sit, the bottom line is that our bottom is on the line. If the chair is not sufficient for the task, then we end up on the floor. In the same way, it is quite possible to believe that God exists, that He is strong enough to save us and that He loves us, and still not place our trust in Him.

This illustrates the three kinds of faith people express toward God, two of which do not result in eternal life. First, there is intellectual faith. This involves giving agreement to a set of facts—acknowledging that there is a God. One might even go on to acknowledge that His Son is Jesus and that Jesus died on the cross to pay for sin, but it is mere intellectual knowledge. The second type of faith people express toward God is called temporal faith, and it takes place when there is a need and a person asks God to meet that need. Once the need is met, this temporary faith is gone. The third and final type of faith, however, is saving faith. This is the word used in the verses we alluded to earlier. This faith is the pisteuo faith in which a person places his or her trust in Jesus Christ as his or her only hope for eternal life. At the moment the person expresses this saving faith toward God, he or she is born again and becomes saved.

Perhaps you've been reading along and you are tired of the nagging doubt that has plagued your mind on this topic for months or years or even decades. Regardless of the reason, you do not have to endure it anymore. I experienced these same doubts as a teenager. I grew up in Corpus Christi, Texas, in an awesome Christian home where my parents took me to church from day one. When I was eight years old, I heard a song about a family in which some of the members ended up in heaven and some ended up in hell. I knew my mom and dad were going to heaven, and I wanted to be with them forever. As a result, my parents took me to see our pastor, and we prayed together to trust Jesus as my Savior.

However, after swimming in lukewarm Christianity through my high school years, I was arrested by God—stopped dead in my tracks. I was sitting in church one day when the speaker challenged every person in the room who believed they were genuinely born again to go back to the moment we trusted him and remember what we said to God. *What did I say to God?* I thought. Did I merely want eternal life, or did I indeed place my trust in Christ at that moment? I honestly could not remember the words I said because it was at such a young age.

The coming months brought doubt, anguish, and many sleepless nights. Finally, I shared my concerns with one of my spiritual mentors, and he said very simply, "Let's pray right now and get it straight." It seemed so simple. I could just pray in that moment and take care of it once and for all? Why had I not done this? I remember even now why I had not settled this issue. I knew that a person can only be born again one time and that is a forever transaction, so I got it in my head that if I prayed about this again, it would be an insult to God, a type of sacrilege. However, one day I heard a simple analogy that clarified this issue for me.

Suppose you have a young son who goes to his first-grade class one day and his classmates tell him that he is not really your son, but you are simply letting him live with you. He becomes distraught and is in emotional turmoil all that day. Now, would you want him to internalize this pain and bottle it up, keeping it to himself? Or would you want him to come and sit on your lap and share this burden? Would you be angry if he did? Would you be disappointed in him for being gullible enough to believe such nonsense, or would you take him in your arms and give him the assurance he so desperately craves? In 1 John 5:13, the writer states that "these things" (the scriptures) have been written that you may know you have eternal life. It is God's will that every believer walks in confident assurance of eternal life. It is Satan's will that every believer doubt his or her eternal life because that is the surest way he can keep us from doing any real damage to his kingdom of darkness.

I bowed my head that day and prayed, with full knowledge of what I was doing, and opened my heart to Christ, placing my trust firmly in Him for eternal life. I have not doubted again in the forty years that have followed. I have often joked with my friends that when I get to heaven, I would like to ask God two questions: (1) Did O. J. Simpson do it alone? and (2) Was I really saved when I was eight or eighteen? The truth is that my spiritual life exploded after gaining assurance of my salvation, and only then did I become a vibrant witness to Christ and His love.

Do you have doubts? Do not entertain them another moment. Bow your head and your heart at this moment, and hammer a stake deep into the ground. Pray this from your heart:

> Dear God, I know You love me and You want to be with me now and forever. I realize that my sin has cut me off from You because You are holy and perfect. I know you died on the cross to pay for my sins, and I turn away from my sin and place my trust in You alone for my eternal life. Come into my life and be my Savior and Lord. Give me the assurance that I am saved and safe forever. Amen.

Now, bask in the grace that He has poured over you as a healing balm for sin. Breathe deeply, knowing he has banished the doubts that Satan has used against you. Never again will you have to wonder; you are saved and safe forever in His hand according to John 10:28.

CHAPTER 4

The Big Picture: The View from Twenty Thousand Feet

There are many reasons why the average follower of Christ does not regularly share Jesus, but I believe many of these reasons can be traced back to a failure to see the big picture of Christ's work in the world. The story is told of a man walking by the construction site where an enormous building was being constructed. As he walked by, he asked one of the brick masons what he was doing, to which he replied, "I'm laying bricks." Walking a bit further, he asked a second mason the same question, "What are you doing?" He replied, "I'm building a magnificent cathedral." One of the workers saw only what was in his hands, what was immediately before him. The other saw the big picture of the ultimate goal of the seemingly menial task at hand.

We often get caught up in the administrivia of life. Focusing on our endless task lists and this daily grind can give us a sort of tunnel vision in which we see only the small picture of our lives. Let's stop and look at sharing Jesus from a different perspective. Depending on the mode of transportation you choose for your family vacation, you will have a completely different view of the journey. If your family drives to Los Angeles from somewhere in the Midwestern United States, you will see people and businesses and parks and vast forests and birds and all manner of things up close and personal. If you travel by train, you are more likely to see more remote areas and fewer people, businesses, and so forth. And if you travel by plane, when you look out your window, you will miss the details but will get a bird's-eye view of the grand landscape. All of these are wonderful ways to travel, each with its own vantage point. I remember just how bored my kids were as we were driving from Houston to El Paso when they were very young. (This was before handheld video games and smartphones.) And who could blame them; there's not much to see. However, I also remember a time when my youngest son was in seventh grade looking out the window of the airplane as we were taking off from Beijing, China, during his first short-term mission trip. He was utterly amazed to see the rivers snaking their way through the landscape and mountains and huge banks of clouds and the sunset from twenty thousand feet.

We would do well to look over the landscape of time and eternity from God's perspective and realize that we are part of what God has been doing from before the world began. A quote from John Piper first jolted me into seeing this truth. He famously says: "Missions exists because worship doesn't."[1]

I still remember reading that statement the first time. It affected me deeply. If the whole world was truly worshiping

---

[1] John Piper, *Let the Nations Be Glad! The Supremacy of God in Missions* (Grand Rapids, MI: Baker, 1993/2003), 17.

the Lord Jesus, then there would be no reason for mission efforts or evangelism of any kind. However, because there are people in evangelized areas who have not bowed, and people in unreached areas who have never heard, we go and share this good news.

We are not simply laying bricks in some random modern art project. We are part of the march of God's glory that is unfolding wave after wave and will continue to unfold until, as the writer of Matthew says, "This Gospel of the kingdom shall be preached in the whole world as a testimony to all the nations, and then the end will come" (Matthew 24:14 NASB). The sooner we realize that we are riding God's wave of glory like a surfer in Hawaii, the sooner we will realize that trying to control it is futile. A surfer doesn't generate the wave, nor does he control it; he simply keeps watch for the right wave and rides it. I love this analogy because sharing Jesus is every bit as exhilarating as surfing, when you see it from God's perspective.

This truth has become more than a theological tenet to me. It fuels my passion for sharing Jesus. It is the promise that in joining God in His work, my life will have meaning and purpose, and in making disciples, God's work through me will continue to the end of time.

It has been said that great men live with the end in view. Knowing the end of the story from the beginning, that the kingdom of God will march on across the planet until the day Jesus brings all things under His feet, gives me confidence in God's ability to work even through a weak vessel like me. This victorious march of God can serve as the lens through which we see the world. It should color our thinking and guide our actions.

The alternative is to focus on my own circumstances, which magnifies my inabilities. Focusing on my circumstances instead of keeping the big picture in mind is a little like focusing on your windshield while you're driving. It's actually pretty deadly because other things (like the white lines on the road) blur, and you could end up on the sidewalk or in the ditch. Looking *through* your windshield, however, keeps the important things in focus. God's desire is to impact this world through you. Keep the big picture in mind, and spend time with Him today. Tell Him your heart's desire is to be used as a conduit for His life to flow into the lives of the thirsty people you will walk by and rub elbows with tomorrow and the next day and the next. That spirit of availability is worth more to God than any amount of unsurrendered ability. Remember, you have the privilege of joining the great God of the universe in fulfilling a plan that cannot fail. That mind-set affords us the opportunity to share Jesus with confidence.

I have also found tremendous courage and confidence to share Christ in the word of God. There are two passages that can inspire us to share with confidence, and they both contain the word *power*. The first of these passages is the great commission found in Matthew 28. It is perhaps the most famous passage in the Bible related to sharing the gospel. It has been interesting to me that so many people only quote verses 19 and 20 when sharing the great commission when verse 18 is an integral part of Christ's last great challenge to us. In its entirety it reads:

"And Jesus came and spake unto them, saying, All power is given unto me in heaven and in earth. Go ye therefore, and teach all nations, baptizing them in the name of the Father and of the Son, and of the Holy Ghost: Teaching them to observe all things whatsoever I have commanded you: and, lo, I am with you always, even unto the end of the world. Amen" (KJV). Without verse 18 we would have no idea what the "therefore" of verse 19 is there for. The meaning is clear: because (and only because) all power in heaven and in earth is in Jesus and Jesus is in us, we have the power to share Jesus. This gives me a confident assurance that when I speak any word of witness regarding the person of Christ, His power is present and active, ensuring that such a word will not return void "powerless" but will go forth in power.

I have many proud moments as a father to three fine young men. However, none surpasses the time when my oldest son came to me to ask if he could go live in China to share the gospel through the ministry of an international missions agency. My heart leapt at the thought that my son had the desire to see people come to know Jesus and that he was willing to invest his life in this noble pursuit. Now, if I can be so touched by my son's obedience to the great challenge of God, imagine the joy that fills our heavenly Father's heart when one of His children steps out in faith to speak His name to someone who needs eternal life. This moves the heart of God even to the point that He would marvel. We know this because only twice in His earthly ministry do we see the Bible state that Jesus "marveled," and both situations had to do with faith. The first is the centurion's faith in Matthew 8, which was so strong that he declared that Jesus did not even need to come to his home to heal his servant but simply speak it and it would be so. The second time he marveled regarding faith was at a lack of faith. Mark 6 tells the story of Jesus coming to his hometown of Nazareth. Because people knew Him as a child, they could not believe He was indeed the Son of God, and the Bible states that He could do only a few miracles because of their unbelief.

When we share Jesus, we should do it with the knowledge that our heavenly Father is intimately interested in what we are doing at that moment and His power is coming to bear on the situation. The outward response of those we share with is irrelevant. Whether they fall on their knees and ask, "What must I do to be saved?" or totally reject the truth, that faithful word has its effect. Just because we can't often measure it with our own natural senses does not mean it's not happening. Before any massive earthquake, there are tremors only detectable to the most sensitive seismic instruments. Our clear instruction is simply to tell the truth about our Savior. The results are not up to us.

For a moment, let's look at the other passage that promises God's power when we share Jesus. Acts 1:8 says, "But you will receive power when the Holy Spirit has come upon you; and you shall be My witnesses both in Jerusalem, and in all Judea and Samaria, and even to the remotest part of the earth" (NASB).

Sharing Jesus with confidence doesn't come from simply learning a gospel presentation and then relying on your personality to deliver it well. Our confidence must come from the power of

God present in our witness. Acts 1:8 promises that when the Holy Spirit comes to live in us that we receive with His indwelling presence a supernatural power and that power is for the purpose of sharing Jesus from wherever we currently live to the ends of the earth.

So, anyone who has the Holy Spirit living in him or her possesses the power of God to be a witness as well. And although there has been confusion surrounding who has the Holy Spirit, the Bible is clear that every true follower of Jesus has the Holy Spirit living in them. Romans 8:9 states, "However, you are not in the flesh but in the Spirit, if indeed the Spirit of God dwells in you. But if anyone does not have the Spirit of Christ, he does not belong to Him" (NASB). So, as a believer you do have the Holy Spirit living in you, and in turn you have the supernatural power that raised Jesus from the dead present in your life as well. But that power is not something we can wield as we see fit for our own purposes. This power can only be used by God through us for His purposes. And since His purpose is to make the name of Jesus famous throughout the earth, then we can be sure that when we join God in that purpose by sharing Jesus His power is present and active at that moment.

It is interesting that in the two passages of scripture mentioned above that there are two very different words used in the original language that can both be translated as "power." The word used in the great commission of Matthew 28 is *eksousia* and is translated in most versions as "authority." This power is the kind of power possessed by a policeman who can stop an eighteen-wheeler simply by turning on his lights and siren or even by stepping out in front of it with his hand held high. When the driver pulls over and stops, he is responding not to one man but to the entire local, state, and federal government that has empowered this policeman. In the same way, when we speak the name of Jesus to someone who has not yet believed, we do so with the blessing and the authority of God Almighty behind us. There is power in the name of Jesus, and when we are led by the Holy Spirit to share Jesus, He has promised that His power will come to bear on the situation at hand. With this in the forefront of our mind, the spirit of timidity melts away, and we share with a confident joy that our efforts are blessed by God and fueled by His matchless authority.

The Greek word used in Acts 1:8 is a very different but equally important one. The word is *dunamis*, from which we get our word for dynamite. This word denotes God's miraculous or "dynamic" power. This power is seen in the healing miracles of Jesus as He walked throughout the land of Palestine encountering people like blind Bartimaeus recorded in Mark 10 and the woman who had a blood disease found in Luke 8. In fact, when the woman with the blood condition touched Jesus and was healed instantly, He stated that "power has gone out of Me." Jesus used this Greek word for power in this instance, indicating that miracle-working power had flowed from Him to this woman. This dynamic power is manifested when God chooses to suspend the normal laws of the universe to accomplish something truly miraculous. And that kind of power is constantly being released by God in situations where His name is shared. It's through this power that men and women, like Saul of Tarsus, are suddenly and irrevocably converted, having their hearts of stone miraculously tenderized so they become vibrant followers of Jesus. And we can see that same resurrection kind of power come alive in our lives if we will simply step out in faith to speak the name of Jesus to someone who does not believe.

After studying these two "powerful" words for some time, it occurred to me that they come together beautifully in the story of the paralytic carried by four friends as recorded in Mark 2. This man was in a desperate condition, and he and his friends knew that only the miraculous power of Jesus could help. They carried him to the home where Jesus was, and because they could not get to Jesus, they climbed on the roof and lowered this man into the presence of Jesus. Upon seeing the man and their faith, Jesus decided, much to their surprise, to unleash His eksousia power by stating, "Your sins are forgiven." These men had carried their friend to Jesus, expecting Him to immediately heal him through the dunamis power, but Jesus showed that the priority was not the body but the soul. So He saved him by His authority as God's Son. Then, once the man's soul was saved, Jesus saw fit to heal him by His dynamic power. I believe that when we understand the true extent of God's power available to those who are faithful witnesses, we will see everyday believers become vibrant witnesses for Christ who get used to seeing God's power manifested in miraculous ways.

My own journey from quiet Christian to excited witness for Jesus was fueled by finally understanding the fullness of God's blessing and power extended to those who simply speak up for

Him. And in those years, it's been the greatest adventure of my life to see the power of God up close and personal in the lives of hundreds who I've had the pleasure of leading to saving faith. One story that illustrates this exposes one of my unique challenges. You see, we all have a certain kind of person we find it hardest to share the gospel with. For some, sharing Jesus hut to hut in Africa sounds daunting. To me it's where I am most comfortable. For some people sharing Christ with bikers and people on the streets is probably scary. But for some reason, the hardest kind of people for me to share with are wealthy, powerful businessmen. And as God would have it, I found myself on a certain day several years ago sitting in the office of a multimillionaire I had befriended over our mutual love for classic cars. I knew beyond a shadow of doubt that God was telling me to share the gospel with him, but I was so intimidated I couldn't seem to get a word out. Then suddenly, this truth took over, and I realized that he was as much in need of the truth as anyone I had ever met.

So I asked him this question: "So, from the looks of your office, it's clear to see that you've traveled the world over. In all your travels, what have you learned about what it takes for a person to go to heaven?"

The next moments are implanted in my memory vividly. He said, "Oh, that's easy; it's all about keeping the golden rule. You keep it and you get in; you don't keep it and you don't get in."

In all my years of asking people questions about eternal life, I don't think I ever heard it put so matter-of-factly … and so wrong. I asked if I could share what God says in His word about eternal life, and after I shared the truth of the gospel, this man prayed so sweetly and so humbly to place his trust in Jesus alone for eternal life.

In that office, on that ordinary day, I knew I had seen the extraordinary power of God perform a miracle greater than a camel going through the eye of a needle. And although I have not always been the faithful witness I should be, I am no longer surprised when I see God melt a human heart in front of my eyes. It's the power that comes from a biblical perspective.

As you see the spread of the gospel over the world from God's perspective and you adopt that as your own view, you will find that God will instill in you a spirit of power, love, and soundness of mind (see 2 Timothy 1:7) that will displace any spirit of fear.

CHAPTER 5

They Are Thirsty

Until recently, our church has made a practice of dropping off a gift to guests who visit our worship services. This is practically unheard of today, but most of the time it was because they expressed an interest in knowing more about our church or about God. Knowing that this was a bit forward, we would simply offer them a quick thank you for being our guest, hand them a gift, and leave. And yet, we were amazed at the number of times they would ask us to come into their homes, and we were equally amazed at how willing they were to discuss spiritual things. To date, over one hundred people have prayed to receive Christ through this ministry. I'll not waste paper debating the pros and cons of this type of ministry, but it does make the point that they are thirsty. If, against all odds and in a practice that is deemed by many to be outdated, we still had over one hundred people invite us in to trust Jesus as Savior, that speaks volumes. It tells me that while church attendance has continued to be in sharp decline among the general population and while our culture continues to race toward being not only post-Christian but anti-Christian, people still wonder about life after death. Don't believe the lie that people don't want to talk about things of eternal significance. They are thirsty.

There is also statistical evidence from studies done in our own nation that people are thirsty. In a recent poll of over one thousand Americans, Zogby International and the Center for Missional Research found that 56 percent of respondents said they do wonder about where they will spend eternity. A whopping 20 percent say they wonder *daily* about this question. When asked, "How often do you wonder, 'How can I find more meaning and purpose in my life?'" remarkably, almost *one in three respondents* wonders about this question daily.

There is one in-home visit I remember vividly. We drove to the inner-city apartment of a single mom whose son had visited one of our children's programs. We knocked on the door and told the woman that we did not want to intrude on her evening but simply wanted to give her a gift and thank her for allowing her son to participate in one of our ministries. She was very friendly and invited us in. We sat and talked with her, and she shared how difficult it was to be a single mom. She was working full-time as a paralegal while also attending college classes at night and raising two children with the help of family. It was apparent that this young lady, whom we will call Michelle, was happy to have us come and offer hope to her in such a difficult situation.

When we turned the conversation to spiritual things, I said, "Michelle, our church really exists to help people to be one hundred percent sure that if they die they will spend eternity in heaven with God. Would you say you are one hundred percent sure?" Her answer was typical. She responded in the negative. But then the conversation took an amazing turn.

Before I share the rest of that story, let me explain something. Each evening before we make these in-home visits, I share something from the word of God to encourage those in attendance. That night I told the story of Philip and the Ethiopian found in Acts 8. Now, there are many points a person could make from that story, but the most encouraging part to me, which I shared that night, was that when Philip ran up to the chariot of this very important man, this man was wondering. His curiosity was piqued. He had traveled from Africa, where he served as the treasurer to Candace the queen of the Ethiopians, to Jerusalem to hear about the God of Israel. Perhaps he had heard of the miracles of Moses—the Red Sea Crossing, the destruction of the armies of Pharaoh, the cloud, the pillar of fire. Maybe he was told of God's promise to Abraham or of the great flood God had brought on the earth in Noah's day.

We do not know what caused him to come, but we do know that he had gone to great lengths to hear about God. We have no doubt that he was wondering because when Philip joined him, the Ethiopian was reading the prophecy concerning the coming of Jesus, and he asked, "Who is the prophet talking about, himself or someone else?" He was sitting there wondering about spiritual things. I shared with my friends how encouraging it was to me that still in our world today people are wondering about spiritual things. It's great to know that we are not out there trying to answer questions that no one ever asks themselves.

Now, back to Michelle. Here's what she went on to say: "You

know, I'm not really sure where I will go when I die, but I have been wondering that ... this week!"

It was all I could do to keep from elbowing my friends and saying, "I told you they were wondering!"

She went on to explain that she had even gone to lunch with a lady that very week and they had talked about this. In fact, the lady had brought it up by asking her if she knew for sure where she would go when she died. When she said this, I immediately assumed that this person she had lunch with must be a fired-up follower of Christ who shared the gospel with her. However, I was amazed when she said, "I told the lady I didn't know for sure, and the lady replied, 'I don't either, but I guess you just have to keep trying.' And now you're here asking me the same thing!" It was a powerful confirmation of the truth we had just discussed. We shared with her how she could have this assurance, and there in her living room, she prayed to trust Jesus alone for her eternal life. People are thirsty for spiritual truth.

Now, I do have to admit that some people are thirstier than others. This is why sometimes we intentionally take the gospel to those who are thirstier For example, the poor are spiritually thirsty because they recognize their need more readily than a person who is financially self-sufficient. Jesus talked about this in Matthew 19:24, "Again I say to you, it is easier for a camel to go through the eye of a needle, than for a rich man to enter the kingdom of God." It's not that God has decided to make it more difficult for someone wealthy to go to heaven. It is simply harder for a wealthy person to admit his or her need and become dependent on God because he or she is not used to depending on others. With that being said, the reality is that the rich man needs God in his life just as desperately, so we also have to take living water to those who may be swimming in the salt water of possessions or wealth where there's "water, water everywhere and not a drop to drink."

We need to be the best drinking fountains we can be. One of the most annoying things in the world is to spot a drinking fountain when you really need it and approach it with anticipation to find that it only squirts a tiny stream or nothing at all. It sits there inviting, available, offering relief. And then you walk up and turn the chrome handle and there's nothing there but a dribble of water with virtually no pressure behind it.

How many people have seen us with a joy and hope they do not possess? How many have come closer to have a look at this living water, wondering if it would quench the thirsty wonderings of their heart, only to find a meager dribble of the reason for the hope that is in us? Some of them even give the handle a tug, just to see what comes out. They say things like, "How can you be so calm when your child is straying?" Some say things like, "I love the way you always see things in a positive light." We sometimes give humble answers like, "That's just the way I was raised," or other responses that are well-intended but absolutely waste tremendous opportunities to give testimony to how we first drank of the very water they now see flowing from our soul. It doesn't mean that we see an opportunity and blast them in the face with pulses from our living water guns.

That would be like taking your flashlight on a dark night

and shining it right in someone's eyes. Yes, there is light, but it's certainly not showing the way. In fact, it's keeping them from seeing the next steps on the path. Surely we can follow the leading of the Spirit and land somewhere between the embarrassed, silent Christian and the super-spiritual scripture spouter. Honestly, we just need to learn to look for signs of thirst and respond with honest and loving truth. The Bible is clear that we must "speak the truth in love" (Ephesians 4:15 NIV). So, the love and the truth are to be proportional. As the love flows, so should the truth, and when the love stops, stop giving out truth! It's amazing what can happen when you pray sincerely and ask God to help you identify "drinkable moments" when a person you are with is showing thirst.

Not only is this thirst in people observable in our everyday lives, but it is also guaranteed by God. Every civilization that has ever been discovered has had some form of worship expressed in the remnants of its culture. These attempts to know or worship or appease God all stem from the thirst God has engineered in us. It should encourage us to share Christ when we read the words of Ecclesiastes 3:11, "He has made everything appropriate in its time. He has also set eternity in their heart" (NIV).

Questions of eternity weave their way in and out of people's minds on a daily basis. When the Bible says that God has "set eternity in their heart," there is an undeniable reference to the "wondering" of humankind throughout the ages about questions of eternal significance. This is the source of Pascal's concept of a "God-shaped hole" in every person's heart.

The power of this truth must not be minimized. Another

reason believers fail to share Christ on a regular basis is because they feel they are forcing their beliefs on uninterested persons. This is simply not the case. A loving answer at a drinkable moment is often welcomed, especially when offered without condescension or condemnation. Test this out in your own life and you will be amazed.

CHAPTER 6

The Power of Inviting

I love the word *invite*. I have always loved that word. When I was in grade school, there was nothing as exciting as when a classmate would have a birthday party and I would get an invitation. It made me feel special that *I* was invited to the party. Now, truth be told, I was most likely invited because their moms were merciful ladies who went out of their way to be sure that the skinniest kid in the school was not forgotten, but regardless, I was invited! There are two invitations in scripture that powerfully depict God's heart for the world. Here is the first:

Then he said to his servants, "The wedding banquet is ready; *go to the street corners and invite to the banquet anyone you find."* So the servants went out into the streets and gathered all the people they could find, both good and bad, and the wedding hall was filled with guests. (Matthew 22:8–10 NIV, emphasis mine)

This passage depicts the normal Christian life. We are to constantly be in an "inviting mode" as we go through life. How we look at this idea of inviting people to Jesus will determine, to a large extent, how we deliver these invitations. If we think

41

that our job is to find people we can enlist to bear the religious burdens we carry, that will come out as we share. Imagine seeing someone weighed down by a backpack full of bricks and then having them come to you and let you know that they have just such a backpack for you! It is true that there will be burdens to bear as we walk with Jesus. I am not advocating that we share a "fairy-tale gospel" that guarantees people that when they trust Jesus for eternal life that everything will be easy. I am saying that if you know Jesus, you must admit that the burdens that come while walking with Jesus pale in comparison to the blessings of knowing Him. The real difference is that some people are spreading religion (the proverbial backpack) and some are sharing real life in Jesus. It's such a blessing to give out invitations to Christ. We were literally chosen by Jesus to issue His invitation to others. What an amazing thing that we are given this honor. And when people open this invitation, they find the very words of Jesus:

> "I, Jesus, have sent my angel to give you this testimony for the churches. I am the Root and the Offspring of David, and the bright Morning Star." *The Spirit and the bride say, "Come!" And let him who hears say, "Come!" Whoever is thirsty, let him come; and whoever wishes, let him take the free gift of the water of life.* (Revelation 22:16–17 NIV)

In this passage, there is an amazing chorus of invitation that starts with the angel (messenger) and moves to the Spirit, the Bride, and even the hearer. Together they are enthusiastically calling anyone and everyone to the gift of living water. This is clearly and simply God's invitation to all humankind to enjoy His salvation. Those who do not yet know Christ are referred to as "those who are thirsty." We have the opportunity to be used by God to invite thirsty people to drink living water. However, if we are to be used by God in this opportunity of inviting, we must be inviting people.

Jesus was such a person. Think about it. Do you really believe that throngs of common people would crowd around a person who was constantly condemning them and pointing out their failures and shortcomings? I don't think so. Jesus was called a "friend of sinners" (Matthew 11:19 NIV). And even those who had much to hide and much to be ashamed of still felt drawn to this inviting man of compassion. This was not because Jesus didn't speak straight truth. At times, He was downright blunt in His speech, but those harsh words were reserved almost exclusively for the religious leaders of the day. (Those who went around giving out backpacks filled with religious bricks.) He condemned their arrogance, and on several occasions, He called them "snakes." In fact, when the religious leaders of the day scolded the people, using the law as a club, Jesus rebuked them and told them they were trying to lay burdens (backpacks) on the backs of people that they themselves refused to carry. If you desire to be an inviting person, you need nothing more than to follow the example of Jesus. Think about the great variety of people who were drawn to him: Pharisees, tax collectors, streetwalkers, and more. It's so interesting that the most pure and holy person who ever walked the planet was also the most approachable to those who were sinners. I believe this was true first and foremost because of the genuine compassion He exuded. But I also believe it was because of what He didn't do. He didn't feel a need to constantly comment on people's behavior or to condemn them. Let's look closer at the life of Jesus as He interacts with a lady who does not know Him, a woman at a well, as recorded in John 4.

The first thing we see is that His very lifestyle was inviting. Not only was His walk with His Father beyond reproach, but He planned His life around those He had come to seek and to save.

Second, Jesus had an inviting personality. This included not only His demeanor right down to His body language but His conversation as well. In His words and actions, He exhibited the fruit of the Spirit at all times.

I remember many years ago sitting in a class in which the teacher asked the following: "Is there someone you know that is truly obnoxious? Do they act as if they are always right? Do they sometimes offer two opinions on the subject at hand?" And then he said, "If you can't think of someone like that, it's probably you!"

Before we take a closer look at the inviting lifestyle and personality of our Savior, let me speak to the way lifestyle and personality work together. It's summed up in this powerful maxim:

> *Your walk gives credibility to your talk,*
> *but*
> *your talk gives clarity to your walk.*

Most of us have heard the famous quote that has been

erroneously attributed to St. Francis of Assisi: "Preach the word at all times and when necessary use words."

No matter who said it (probably the great philosopher "Anonymous"), this quote creates an unnecessary division between living out the gospel and proclaiming it.

The gospel, according to Romans 10:14, is necessarily verbal. It clearly states, "How, then, can they call on the one they have not believed in? And how can they believe in the one of whom they have not heard? And how can they hear without someone preaching to them?"

During my years on church staff as a mission pastor, I often marveled at how willing people were to do service projects that did not involve sharing the gospel. And while I fully understood and we often practiced the principle of serving others to win a hearing for the gospel, we sometimes just don't get around to sharing the clear message of salvation.

I heard a very convicting statement at one point that guided my mission projects thereafter: "If I serve others and do not share the gospel, they will think well of me. If my service to others opens the door and I share the gospel, they will think well of Jesus."

If I have been walking with Jesus, the talk I do about Him will have anointed power. But it's through clear words that people will understand how to say yes or no to His offer of eternal life.

We see in Jesus a stellar example of being a living invitation. In the famous story of John 4, we immediately see His inviting lifestyle. His sinless, holy life gave His words incredible power. No matter what He talked about, He had lived it out flawlessly, and that gave His message great credibility. Jesus was already well into His year of popularity where He was often thronged with great masses of people. Yet, an amazing facet of Jesus's encounter with the woman at Jacob's Well is that He literally planned His schedule around this singular person who needed him.

In fact, as the story of this encounter is recorded in the fourth chapter of John, verse 4 is a curious one. It simply says, "Now he had to go through Samaria."

What makes this interesting is that the route through Samaria is not the only way to get from Judea to Galilee. In fact, it was not the suggested route. Jews carefully avoided it because of their disdain for Samaritans. The Jews hated them because, in their view, the Samaritans had polluted not only the bloodline by intermarriage but the religion of Judaism as well. And yet, for some reason, He "needed" to go through Samaria. The reason He needed to go there was to connect with this woman who would become instrumental in reaching her entire village with the gospel.

I've given this some thought, and I am so glad that I was not the disciple in charge of His itinerary. Because, if so, I might have argued hard against leaving the masses to minister to the one. I would have probably argued that for the "greater good," we should find a large hill and provide a free meal and cover more territory by preaching to thousands.

I might have argued that if we must leave Judea and go to Galilee that at the very least we should take the safer route through Perea and avoid that godforsaken land of Samaria.

But Jesus planned His life around one lost woman that day.

He knew His father had set a divine appointment for Him at a well, and He always did what His father had planned for Him.

This is true of each of us. God has laid out divine appointments with those who do not yet know Him, and He will use us to bring them to faith.

If we are not intentional about engaging people, we can become like the monks of centuries past. Even as the monks retreated from the world into a Christian cacoon, we too can get to where we live in a Christian bubble, spending 95 percent of our time with those who believe. And in so doing, we become salt that has lost it saltiness or salt that never makes it out of the shaker.

When you consider the love of Christ for the world, one beautiful facet of that love is that He entered our world. Any father who wants to love his son will enter his world even if that means video games or tuba lessons. Any husband who truly loves his wife knows that at times he must enter her world through antique shopping or taking a long walk even when that's not his greatest interest. If we are going to become effective witnesses, we must make time to engage people who have not yet trusted Christ in saving faith.

We are to be *in* the world but not *of* it. While Jesus does say, "You are not of the world" (John 15:16), which emphasizes that our lifestyle is to be different from the sinful patterns of this world, He does not command or condone retreat from the battle for souls.

In fact, Paul bluntly states this in 1 Corinthians 5:9–11, where he says,

I wrote to you in my epistle not to keep company with sexually immoral people. Yet I certainly did not mean with the sexually immoral people of this world, or with the covetous or extortioners or idolaters, since then you would need to go out of the world. But now I have written to you not to keep company with anyone named a brother, who is sexually immoral or covetous or idolater or a reviler or a drunkard or extortioner not even to eat with such a person. (NIV)

So this verse, the strongest warning in the New Testament regarding keeping bad company, only warns against spending time with those who claim to be followers of Christ but live an unholy lifestyle. So as we live out our faith in front of those who do not yet know Christ, we must be different enough to make them thirsty but gentle enough not to be condescending or condemning. We need to be "surprisingly normal." It's been so fun to meet people in the daily rhythm of life and have them be quite surprised when they find out that I am a devoted follower of Jesus. The expectation of the world often is that devoted followers of Jesus have to be "odd for God" to the point that they are boring or unapproachable.

If Jesus was anything, He was approachable. But Jesus not only had an inviting lifestyle. He had an inviting personality as well.

It's not enough to just be around those who do not yet know Christ. Once we enter their world, we need to exude the love of

Jesus in clear and powerful ways, and we need to speak clearly about the source of our joy.

We must avoid Satan's trap of being that judgmentally outspoken person. A person can be spiritually obnoxious even by the way he or she quotes the Bible. This doesn't mean we sell out and compromise our conviction about sharing the gospel. It does mean we don't try to force steak down a baby's throat and we don't expect lost people to think, talk, or act like followers of Jesus.

In talking with the woman at Jacob's Well, Jesus stepped over several huge cultural barriers that had been carefully constructed through years of conflict and tradition. While even traveling through Samaria, as a Jew, was quite abnormal in His day, talking with this particular woman smashed through several additional walls.

Some years after the kingdom of Israel was divided into the Northern Kingdom (Israel) and the Southern Kingdom (Judah), the Northern Kingdom was conquered by the Assyrians. Foreigners (Gentiles) were brought in to settle this area, and the Israelites began to intermarry with them. This was forbidden by God because of their false gods, and soon there were idols set up in the holy cities of Dan and Bethel.

Because of this polluting of worship and the intermarriages, the Jews of the Southern Kingdom began to hate those in the area of Samaria. Years later, when some forty thousand plus Jews were allowed to return to Jerusalem to rebuild the city, the Samaritans opposed them and did their best to hinder the rebuilding of the wall and the city. For this, too, they were hated by the Jews.

Still, Jesus spoke with compassion to this Samaritan. That should have been strike one against Jesus approaching this woman. But not only was she a Samaritan—she was a woman. Women in the time of Jesus were considered property. Generally speaking, women were to be seen and not heard, and rabbis were not to taint their reputation by consorting with them. In fact, history records that many Jewish men would start their prayer time each day by praying, "Oh, Lord, I thank You that You did not create me a slave, a gentile, or a woman!"

And finally, as if these were not enough, strike three was that she was an immoral woman. We find out later in the conversation that the man she was living with was not her husband and that she had already had five other men. It was also remarkable that she came to get water at noon. The custom of women was to get water in the morning before the heat of the day, and this was the highlight of a woman's day because the well was the place where they socialized. This woman came at noon precisely to avoid this interaction. She was even ostracized by the Samaritans!

And yet Jesus, in His own inviting way, not only spoke to her gently but was willing to drink after her! When considered carefully in the light of these cultural mores, this encounter is nothing less than astounding.

I will never forget a conversation with a man who was part of our witness training course. We were midway through the semester, and I had shared this principle of crossing barriers to share the gospel. He shared that the week before he had gone on a business trip and upon arriving at one airport for a layover, he began to look for a chair in the crowded gate area when a certain man caught his eye. We will call him Bill. It's important for you to know that this member of our church was the most ultra-conservative, even fundamentalist man among us. And as he tells the story, he saw one open seat in the terminal. The problem was that this open seat was next to a mammoth sized, leather-wearing, inked up guy with a huge wallet tethered to his belt by a large silver chain. He recoiled at the thought of sitting by this man but remembered this lecture on John 4. A fierce mental debate ensued, and finally he admitted that he had categorically decided that he could not and would not associate with such a person. Ashamed at his gut reaction, he forced himself to take the seat and found the man to be not only approachable but quite charming. And while the man did not pray to trust Jesus as Savior that day, he was able to point him the right direction.

We all have, in the back of our minds, profiles of the kind of person with whom we think we cannot interact. And if we do not call them out and deal with them, then we run the risk of categorically denying huge sections of the population the ability to hear the good news.

I shared my own category in an earlier chapter, admitting that I have a very hard time sharing the gospel with wealthy businessmen.

What's your category? If you ask God to reveal it to you, I assure you the Holy Spirit will put His finger on it. I have learned to ask the Lord to help me see people the way He did: simply as someone in need of a touch from God. I have also asked the Lord to make me blind to the external characteristics of people. Someone wisely warned me many years ago, "The worst kind of heart disease is the hardening of the categories." Categorizing people into neat little compartments based on your own biases will only limit how God can move through your life.

Another thing we notice about Jesus as He interacts with this woman in the story told in John 4 is that He started the conversation with a neutral topic and moved to the spiritual. He did not start the conversation at the end. He could have easily met her and immediately said, "You have had five men, and the one you are with now is not your husband." Or He could have started the whole encounter off with the spiritual maxim, "God is a spirit and those who worship Him must worship Him in Spirit and in truth."

But Jesus, being such an inviting personality, simply asked her for a drink. While I realize that the success of our witness is not dependent on slick talk (Paul said, "I do not speak to you with eloquence"), it is important to approach people in an approachable way! We do not see Jesus spouting spiritual truths or even quoting scripture without taking into consideration the life context of His hearers. When we look more closely, we see how this greeting was truly shocking to the woman. Jesus, the one who spoke the universe into existence with His Father, was humbly asking for this woman to meet His need for a drink of water. The attitude our words and body language convey determines to some extent how open people will be to the message we bring. People have a sort of emotional radar and can detect nuances of arrogance, pride, and condescension. These things cause them to raise their defense shields and shut down their spiritual receptors.

This concept is so true that one of the greatest ways you can open avenues to share the gospel is to allow them to speak into your life on a matter where they are somewhat of a subject expert. Whether it's just letting them share the information with you or allowing them to give you hands-on help with some project you are working on, you will be amazed at how this opens a door for the gospel.

I was talking with my dad about this recently, and he affirmed this rarely practiced principle. He stated that some of his greatest friendships had developed very late in life after he and my mom had lost their ability to drive and they began to let others come alongside them and help them. My dad and mom are two of the godliest people I have ever met. He has been leading people to Jesus for over sixty years and has taught Sunday school for over forty years, and during that time, he has touched a lot of lives. At the same time he has been fiercely independent. But now that he is over eighty years old and suffers from macular degeneration and has a hard time getting around, his ministry is flourishing because of this principle. He shared that recently while he and my mom were at church on a Sunday morning, he had a bad spell and almost fell due to his low blood pressure. Fortunately, he sat down and after some rest was able to be taken back home. There was a lady present who asked if she could help. Normally my dad would refuse the help. But because he wanted to build a relational bridge to her, he allowed her to come to the house and help them out with some menial tasks. She went to work cleaning and straightening the house and cooking for them. Later he called her to where he was resting and had the opportunity to talk with her about the Lord. As it turns out, she was already a follower of Jesus but had been in desperate need of encouragement as she was a recovering drug addict. My dad remarked that there was little to no chance that he would have had such an open door had it not been for this girl serving him and my mom.

I cannot tell you how many times I have entered a conversation about cars, and in allowing people who know and love them to teach me something, I have watched them totally open the door to talking about stuff they would have otherwise shut down in five seconds. In fact, I have personally seen people bow their heads and put their trust in Jesus alone in garages and shops and driveways. And in many cases, it was because they simply felt comfortable that this was not a case of a sermon to be delivered but a joy to be shared with a friend.

A case in point may help. I had gone to a transmission shop near my house. I was in the process of fixing up an old Jeep Wrangler that had a very uncooperative manual transmission. I went by this transmission shop and introduced myself and asked a couple of questions, and the next thing I knew, this very friendly shop owner was explaining all about my synchronizers not allowing the proper spin down of the gears—and on and on. I hired him to rebuild my transmission, and every few days I went by to check the progress. Each time he took the time to show me his progress, including the parts he was replacing.

Through this we developed a friendship. Finally, it came up that I was a pastor, and this didn't seem to bother him. In fact, he began to share that his business was not doing very well and asked if I would pray a blessing over his shop. I agreed to do so. He was so thrilled with this prospect that he planned an elaborate barbecue lunch and invited all his tech guys and even invited all the guys from the general mechanic's shop next door. I got to pray over his shop and in the process shared God's plan for eternal life. When the lunch/blessing was over, I got in my car and started to leave the parking lot when I felt a strong impression from the Lord to go back and talk with John. I went back and asked if he had thought about what I said that day regarding eternal life. He said that he had already been thinking about how he needed to get his life straight with God. I prayed with John that day in his office at the front of the shop. At that point, he asked me if I would leave some business cards with him on the desk so he could give them to people who needed prayer. I became the chaplain of the transmission shop that day. About a week later I went by the shop on my day off just to say hello, and John's fiancé was there working the desk. I started talking to her, and she thanked me for helping John get his life right. I shared that it wasn't my coaching but his new relationship with Jesus, and that day Joy prayed to receive Christ. A few months later, I had the privilege of performing John and Joy's wedding. At the wedding, I met John's daughter from another marriage. After the wedding I shared with Sherry, John's daughter, and she prayed to receive Christ. Some months later, Sherry got engaged and wanted me to do her wedding. She and her fiancé came to my office, and in the process of premarital counseling, her fiancé prayed to receive Christ! I have come to expect to see God do amazing things, but even so, I was in awe of what God accomplished with what started as a simple conversation about a transmission.

One very important thing I have learned through this process is to be listening for a neutral topic that can lead to a spiritual conversation. For most people cars won't be the topic that opens the conversation. But if you ask the Lord to open your ears and your heart to hear them, you will find openings into conversations that can easily and naturally move toward eternal things.

It may be in financial issues, marital problems, or concerns they have about their children. Learning to lean into these areas can open a door for relational bridge building that flows right into sharing the gospel.

But Jesus did not stop there. If we simply commiserate with people and basically leave it at "life is tough," then we've done them a huge disservice. Jesus turned the conversation from the physical to the spiritual. The subject at hand was not really water … it was thirst. Jesus took the subject of physical thirst and used it to move the conversation to a deeper kind of thirst, the thirst this woman had in her soul.

It would be easy to say, "This was different because Jesus knew her thoughts!" But if you will stop and think about it, we know their hearts as well. We know there is a void there that can only be filled by Jesus. We know they experience that same thirst felt by the woman with whom Jesus was talking. People are thirsty. They are thirsty for love; they are thirsty for relief; they are thirsty for comfort, for security, for answers.

When America was largely an agricultural society, it was easy to get people to church because the church was the center of social life for farming communities. However, as society changed and people's social lives no longer revolved around the church, we have had to work harder and harder to maintain relevance.

And while concerts and other entertainment-related events are failing to attract people, there is one constant that will not change. If you offer help where people are hurting, they will come. We call them the big three topics: tell people how to better manage their money, and they will come; tell people how to get along with their spouse better, and they will come; and finally, tell them how to raise good kids, and they will come.

What's true for churches is also true for individual followers of Jesus when it comes to sharing the gospel. If you want to draw people into your circle of influence, offer them help and/or prayer in these areas. When you are in daily conversations with people you would like to share Christ with, keep this in mind. It's not as hard as you might think to take a conversation about failing finances and turn it by saying something like, "We realized a long time ago that our financial freedom doesn't depend on Wall Street." To the hurting mom whose child is going off the deep end, you can confess, "We realized a long time ago that we don't have the wisdom to raise our kids alone."

There are so many things about how Jesus interacted with this woman that should guide how we talk with those who are not in Christ. Jesus models here beautifully the passage of scripture found in Colossians 4:5–6, which says, "Be wise in the way you act toward outsiders; make the most of every opportunity. Let your conversation be always full of grace, seasoned with salt, so that you may know how to answer everyone."

Jesus followed the "grace and salt" principle. First, His speech was full of grace. The word *gospel* means "good news." So in sharing truth with others, it naturally follows that we begin with good news. While I agree that before a person can be saved, he must know that he is lost, I do not believe that means that we need to begin every witness encounter by immediately telling the person that he or she is a lying, thieving adulterer. Jesus's first words about the offer of living water were full of grace. She could feel His compassion, and she longed for a way to quench this thirst she had felt deep in her soul. But He didn't stop there. He went from grace to salt when He talked with her about her relationships with men. His words were direct and truthful. While being compassionate He did not compromise the truth. Likewise, however unpopular it becomes to share the truth of the gospel, we must speak the truth in love. We cannot ever fall into the cesspool of liberal theology that says that we are all seeking different roads to heaven. As loving as we may want to be, people must come away knowing that rejecting Jesus is rejecting the only way to a relationship with God and the only way to eternity with Him.

In learning to share the gospel, we can't be duped into believing that the results somehow depend on how smoothly we present it or how well we articulate the truth. However, it is important for us to learn how to present the gospel in a way that the only stumbling block for someone is the stumbling block of truth.

In 1 Peter 2:7–8 the Bible states, "Now to you who believe, this stone is precious. But to those who do not believe, 'The stone the builders rejected has become the cornerstone,' and, 'A stone that causes people to stumble and a rock that makes them fall'" (NIV).

This reminds us that when we share the gospel, some will accept the truth, but for others, the radical truth that Jesus is God and is the only way to heaven will become something they cannot accept. This is just a fact of life, and we must not tamper with the message to try and make it palatable for people. It is what it is. However, the goal is that our words, mannerisms, or lifestyle will not become a stumbling block to someone with whom we share. We should work hard to say things in such a way that it does not cause people to put up their defenses because of their past baggage. Let the only rock of offense be the truth.

I have a wonderful Jewish friend. We've lived in the same neighborhood for years. We bonded as we raised our kids together, particularly through the teen years, his girls and my boys. The trials of raising teenagers was something easy to bond over. Through the years I would ask for legal advice, since he is an attorney, and I helped to keep his kids' bikes and eventually their cars running. Through allowing him to help me and through helping him, we developed a solid friendship. Along the way I have shared Jesus with him on several occasions. I knew he rejected Jesus's claim to be the Messiah, and there was a huge temptation to simply keep things on a superficial plane and only talk about the Old Testament. But on two occasions I have passionately pleaded with him not to reject Jesus. I have also been very honest about the consequences of doing so. I have to admit that these conversations were difficult and amounted to several withdrawals from my relationship account with him. However, I realized that to fail to lay this out in certain terms was to amen his journey to hell. I have learned that so many followers of Jesus are willing to do outreach, meaning to give a cup of cold water in Jesus's name, and many are willing to witness or give a positive word about God, but few are equipped to do evangelism. True evangelism is sharing the gospel in a way that a person has the opportunity to say yes or no to Jesus. Up to now he has clearly said no, but I am holding on to hope that I will see him in glory. If we are to be fishers of men, let's learn to draw the net once it is cast.

Another facet of the way Jesus interacted with this woman was something He didn't do. He didn't focus on theological arguments. Many of the people we will speak to about Jesus have some religious background or experience with a church. Even if they do not have direct experience, most have read or seen something in the media they did or didn't like that they now identify with religion and thereby attribute to God. Because of this caricature of God in their minds, they will often ask questions or even want to argue about issues related to those impressions.

This woman in John 4 brought out her religious baggage and unpacked it in front of Jesus by asking about the proper location of worship. After the conquest of the Assyrians and the ensuing resettlement of the area, the Samaritans went so far as to erect their own temple of worship. This was a complete abomination in the eyes of God and of every God-fearing Jew. Now this lady asked Jesus which temple was the correct one. What a perfect launching pad for a theological tirade. I'm reminded of what Jesus said when cleansing the temple of the money changers, "Passion for My father's house consumes me." Jesus certainly possessed enough passion for and knowledge about this subject to spend the next hour giving an explanation of the historical facts and theological ramifications of such horrific false worship. But He didn't. Instead, He modeled this maxim of evangelism: "The main thing is to keep the main thing the main thing." In fact, what Jesus did was to remind her that it was not about the externals of religion but about the Spirit. We do not know for sure why this lady brought this up at this point. Perhaps she was sincerely confused and needed this explanation to take her next steps in faith. But there is another possibility I would like to posit. It could be that Jesus had hit a nerve in asking about the man she was currently with. And it's possible that when the conversation got personal that she sought to divert attention away from her issues by bringing up religion. I have experienced this on many occasions. I will often find myself in a deeply personal conversation about Jesus when all of a sudden, the person will ask me what seems like an off-the-wall question about the heathen in Africa or whether God can make a rock too heavy for Him to lift. Sometimes it's about the latest doomsday preacher who has set a date for the end of the world. In many cases I have discerned that this is a smokescreen that the person is knowingly or unknowingly throwing up to derail what has become a convicting conversation. On a very rare occasion, I admit that the Spirit has led me to go ahead and do my best to answer the question, but mostly I have learned to say three of the most important words in personal evangelism, "I don't know!"

Contrary to our Western mind-set, we don't need to have all the answers. And although in our minds we figure that not having the answer to a question might totally undermine our credibility with the person to whom we are speaking, that's simply not true. In reality, it's kind of endearing to meet someone who doesn't pretend to have all the answers. By the way, pretending to have all the answers is one of the quickest ways to destroy the credibility needed for an authentic witness. In teaching witness training classes for many years now, I see great relief come across the faces of students as they realize they are not expected to become theological experts before sharing Jesus. And it's freeing to be asked a hard question and to simply say, "I don't know much about that, but could I share something I do know and then if you still have that question you can feel free to ask me then?" This keeps the train right on track and keeps the main thing the main thing. Jesus modeled this beautifully by keeping the main issue front and center. The main issue was, and is today, the true identity of Jesus, and He removes all doubt when He gives perhaps his clearest declaration in the entire New Testament that He is the Messiah. Do not doubt the fact that when you are sharing Christ and you begin to feel insecure or inadequate that oftentimes this is a ploy of Satan to shut down the powerful message of the gospel that is about to break through in someone's life. We can turn this weapon on the devil and use it against him if we allow those feelings of inadequacy to make us more dependent on God.

You may have noticed the peculiar phrasing I suggested earlier, "I don't know much about that, but could I share something I do know and then if you still have that question you can feel free to ask me then?" We need to be careful of what we say if we are to maintain credibility. If you say, "I will answer that later," then you had better have a very good answer when later comes because you have effectively made a promise. If the question was a smokescreen, the person will lose interest in it altogether by the time you finish sharing the gospel and then there is no need to answer the question.

Of course, there are occasions when the person will indeed ask the question again at some point in the conversation, which shows that this was not a smokescreen but truly something that is hindering his or her next steps with God. When that happens, I usually say, "You know, I don't want to just offer up a half-baked answer to such an important question. Can I study that and get back to you?" In so doing, you have shown honor to their question and you've left the door wide open to continue this spiritual discussion.

By the end of this amazing story of the woman at the well, we see the incredible results of Jesus's encounter. This Samaritan woman was never the same. The quality and the direction of her life was radically altered. And that is the story of millions of people in this world who have heard the gospel and embraced Christ.

This should give us the encouragement and confidence to share Christ with others. We know how He changed our lives, and we realize that the possibilities of this change flowing into the lives of others are endless and unimaginable. One person who truly comes to saving faith in Jesus can break through chains of bondage within a family and begin a spiritual legacy that lasts for generations.

In closing out our discussion of the woman at Jacob's Well, it is wonderful to realize that she immediately became a witness. Without any formal training and still theologically inept, she went into her city and told them about this man Jesus. The result is phenomenal. At their request, Jesus stayed two days in that city, and the story ends with two wonderful statements. First, "Many of the Samaritans from that town believed in Him because of the woman's testimony" and second, "We no longer believe just because of what you said; now we have heard for ourselves, and we know that this man really is the Savior of the world."

At first glance, it seemed that this whole episode was about one woman only, when God's heart was for the city. Isn't it true that God operates on so many levels that it is impossible to foresee the scope of His work?

CHAPTER 7

Just Be Jesus in the Moment

The clear and simple message of the gospel cannot be improved upon. God's message to us, like God Himself, is powerful and unchanging, and His word is one of the few things in this world that we are promised will endure for eternity. However, while the message is unchanging, the method of delivery does, and should. For example, when we travel to other cultures, we often change our approach to sharing the gospel to fit the cultural context of the hearers. On one mission trip to China, we did classroom presentations in universities. We found that a dramatic presentation of the prodigal son was especially effective because in Chinese culture, bringing shame on your family is unthinkable. When we were sharing the gospel in Zambia, we used the story of two spiritual kingdoms because in Zambian culture, stories are very important and everything that happens in life is thought to have a spiritual cause.

The need to contextualize the gospel in other cultures highlights the fact that different circumstances call for different methods of sharing Christ. Not only differences in culture but other factors, such as the nature of our relationship with someone, can make one way of explaining the good news more effective than another. Telling someone your salvation story may be exactly what is needed in a given situation. In another context you may use an illustration. And sometimes you will find yourself in a relaxed environment with the time to share a fuller Gospel presentation. All these approaches are valuable because the situation dictates the method.

There is no one-size-fits-all approach to sharing Jesus! This concept is so essential because people are in such different places in their openness to receive the truth, and the Lord always leads us to share Christ in keeping with that level of openness. One of the major cell phone providers used to have a television commercial in which people carrying cell phones were pictured with signal strength bars over their heads as they went about the normal activities of the day. More bars meant more connectivity to their respective provider. I thought about how nice it would be if God would allow us to see a bar graph of a person's spiritual receptivity just above his or her head. With this graph hovering over their head, we could know how open they are to the gospel, and we could then find the ones with full bars and go straight to them. Sounds like a good idea, but in reality, the result would be catastrophic. How do you suppose that those with full bars got to that point? And why is it more important to speak to those who are closest to being born again? Those who are the most open to hearing the gospel most likely got to that place through a number of encounters with believers who were willing to be Jesus to them. In Acts

10:35 the Bible states that "God is no respecter of persons." If we walked past those with little or no connectivity quotient in favor of those who are "closer to knowing God," we would suddenly become "a respecter of persons" and find ourselves in the position of putting a higher or lower value on one soul over another, which is contrary to the words of 1 Timothy 2:3–4, "This is good and acceptable in the sight of God our Savior, who desires all men to be saved and to come to the knowledge of the truth."

Like any civilized people in any corner of the world, our tendencies arise from our culture. We Americans thirst for successful results in all our endeavors. But as flawed people, our definition of success is at times fleshly and warped. There is little doubt that our desire to see every person immediately pray to trust Jesus as Savior comes from a godly motive. However, it is also possible that we still measure our effectiveness by the type of outward response of others to that witness. Herein lies the problem.

Imagine for a moment this ridiculous scene: God is on His throne, looking down on you as you share the gospel with a person who is in despair. The person hears the word and is moved to tears but does not express saving faith in Jesus at that moment. Now imagine God wringing His hands, all the while lamenting that if only you had done better, this person might have been saved. How ludicrous it is to think of God's eternal plan hinging on the power of our personality. We must become comfortable with the idea that as long as we are available and surrendered to be Jesus to someone in word and deed, it is irrelevant whether they move from zero bars of connectivity to one or from one bar to two or whether the eternal connection is locked in at that moment. We must get to the place where we realize that in any of these situations, we have been wildly successful if we have followed the promptings of His Spirit in us.

There is a mission-sending agency that has been responsible for thousands of college students going on short-term foreign mission trips. As a part of their training, at one point they bring a large chain into the room with many links. Somewhere on this chain there is a link that has been painted bright red. The red link is representative of when a person trusts Jesus for eternal life. All the other links are encounters where someone gave a witness of some type before the person was ready to receive Christ. If even one of those links is missing, the chain is broken. The more accurate picture in heaven is of the Father's smile when we say a kind word in passing, when we pray for a coworker's sick child, when we, in some small way, influence a person toward our God. Our hearts need to line up with the heart of God at this point. It is no more spiritual, no more of a blessing to the heart of God, for me to be the harvester in the field of God than it is to plant seed or water it.

The Apostle Paul reminds us in 1 Corinthians 3:6–8,

> I planted, Apollos watered, but God was causing the growth. So then neither the one who plants nor the one who waters is anything, but God who causes the growth. Now he who plants and he who waters are one; but each will receive his own reward according to his own labor. (NIV)

There is a fantastic reward awaiting faithful witnesses both in this life and when we meet the Lord, but there is no mention of a "harvester reward" or a "planter reward" or a "waterer reward" because the reward is equal. That is made clear in these verses: "Now he who plants and he who waters are one …" The reward in this life is seeing changed lives and the wonder that comes from blessing the Father's heart. The prize in eternity is to lay more at the Father's feet for the glory of His Son.

Just be Jesus in the moment and let God take care of the rest.

CHAPTER 8

Build a Bridge Across the Street

During the last few decades, we have seen an urban phenomenon known as "cocooning." People in neighborhoods have increasingly become more and more isolated. Many Americans live in a gated community where they enter their car each day in the privacy of their own garage, go to work, and return to their garage, close the door, and exit the car without ever having to interact with anyone in the neighborhood. This makes it increasingly difficult to reach out to them with the truth of the gospel, which is the real reason God has placed you in your neighborhood. The most effective and natural way to share Jesus is of course to spend time with people, to invest in their lives and earn the right to speak with them about spiritual matters. But gone are the days when this will happen naturally as we all sit on the porch and drink tea and lemonade. Getting to know your neighbors will take intentionality and a plan.

To be the salt and light God called us to be, we are going to have to build bridges across the street to intersect with people. There is a church close to my home that owned property on two sides of a very busy street. On one side sat their sanctuary and on the other was their family ministry building. Obviously, it would be dangerous and impractical to have families walking across the street, so they undertook the massive task of building a bridge across the street. It is a beautiful steel and glass structure. I can only imagine what it took to accomplish this mammoth feat. The permit process alone must have been a nightmare. The planning and costs associated with such a bridge would also be substantial. And yet, it was important to them, and they got it done. That's what churches and individuals do; they do what's important. And when sharing Jesus with our neighbors becomes really important to us, we will adjust the flow of our lives to intentionally intersect with them.

Have you given much thought to why some people just seem to bring other people into the church and even into the kingdom of God so easily and others struggle to accomplish this? It's easy to chalk this up to their "gift of gab" or exuberant personality, but there's likely another reason. The person you admire who seems to bring people to Christ has not only surrendered at some point to be available to God but also has made a decision to dedicate his or her time, talent, and resources to being a bridge builder. Very few of my friends know their neighbors' first names. Even fewer know their neighbors' last names. And even fewer of them ever really spend any time with them. Busyness has pushed the very people we are responsible for out of our lives. And it happens not only in our neighborhoods but in our workplaces and our extended families. Sometimes the churches we belong to plan so much at the church that there is little margin left in our schedule to build bridges of relationship within any of these spheres of influence.

A good starting point for relational bridge building is to stop for a moment and list all the hats you wear in life. I did this and was amazed to find that I am a husband, a dad, a son, a brother, a pastor, a neighbor, a coworker, a mentor, an uncle, a nephew, a cousin, a teacher, and a classic car enthusiast. Do this simple exercise starting with the relationships closest to you, and you will discover the arenas of life in which there are varying chasms between you and members of that group, and you will uncover unlimited opportunities for bridge building.

Now, simple mathematics dictates there is not time to build bridges of friendship and caring to every person in these arenas. However, the beauty is that with so many possibilities, we need only take time to lay the first brick here and there and we will be amazed at how often people will reciprocate by laying the next brick themselves. Also, to be successful, we need to realize that those who do not lay that next brick are not necessarily making a comment on our value. They are just in many other people's circles of influence as well and may be responding to someone else.

It's been thirty years since I sat in a college classroom. While much of what I learned at that small Baptist college influenced my ministry, very few lectures have stayed with me. There is one. I remember a part of that lecture almost word for word because if its powerful impact on my life. Here's an excerpt: "God has endowed every one of us who possess His Spirit with the power to bless. We can best put ourselves in a position to lift up the fallen, the wounded, the hurting by plugging them into the power of God that currently resides in us as believers."

Those simple words clicked with me that day. One reason those words imbedded so deeply that day is because at that time God had put someone in my life who exemplified that to a tee. I met Rodney in Greek class. I think he could tell I was having a hard time grasping the material, and although he was breezing through it, he took time to help me. I had always been a good student and went through school with relative ease, but this particular class had my number, and I wasn't sure I was going to get through it. The fact that he took time for me and invited me to his dorm room for mentoring sessions and hung out with me left a deep impression. In fact, we became fast friends and are still close friends to this day, having encouraged each other through the years as we raised six boys between our two families. Rodney took time for me when he had nothing to gain from the experience except true friendship, and it opened me up for a wealth of spiritual truth he has poured into me since those early college days.

Following that lecture, I began to see that I had spent an inordinate amount of my time on this earth looking for people who would meet my needs, who would mentor me, who would heal my hurt. That day, God began to turn my focus outward. I began to ask very different questions: Whose need can God meet through me? Whom can I mentor? Whose hurt does God want me to help heal?

The beautiful thing I have discovered about this kind of bridge building is that I am not the engineer or the architect of such a project. I am not even the mason, but the mason's apprentice. You see, bridge building involves an architect and an engineer to design the project in such a way that it will sustain the stress of load bearing and a construction company to execute on those plans.

On rare occasions, the architect and engineer are one and the same. This was the case with the world-famous Brooklyn Bridge. The bridge's total length surpasses 5,900 feet, and it boasts a width of 85 feet. The clearance from road bed to water is 135 feet at midspan. This project would have been an astounding feat in any era, so it is spectacular that it was conceived and engineered in the late 1800s by one man: John Augustus Roebling. Not only was this brilliant man the architect and engineer, but he was also designated to oversee the actual construction of the bridge, which he did until his death, when his own son, Washington Roebling, took charge and saw the project to completion by 1883.

I find an interesting parallel here. In Philippians 1 the apostle Paul reminds us, "He who began a good work in you will carry it on to completion until the day of Christ Jesus" (Philippians 1:6 NIV). God is the architect, engineer, and builder of our lives. God does not leave the plans to our own hands to complete but has given us His Son's constant presence through the Holy Spirit. Even the desire to have an outward focus begins with God. In Philippians 2 Paul writes, "It is God who works in you, both to will and to work for his good pleasure" (Philippians 2:13 NIV). Notice the phrasing, "both to will and to work." Both the desire to do God's will and then the power to accomplish it flow from God Himself.

If we will simply approach each day with a listening heart and ministry eyes, He will show us an opening and lay the first brick. As that brick is put in place, God shows us where to lay just one more and then one more. It's reassuring to me that God is the architect, engineer, and builder because He sees the big picture (the architectural drawings) while also being familiar with the most minute detail.

This is where we enter the picture as the mason's apprentice. We're not required to see the entirety of the plans. We are simply handed a brick and told where to place it. And in the end, when this beautiful structure spans the river and there is a grand opening, the plaque at the base of the bridge does not bear the name of the apprentice. It always displays the name of the architect/engineer. It's all about making the name of Jesus famous. Lay the first brick across your street; God will guide you, and He will get the glory in the end.

During my most recent mission trip to Zambia, Africa, I had some amazing discussions with the volunteers. Each of them had trained for a couple of months to share the gospel in order to be used by God to plant a new church. Each day, as they went hut to hut, their confidence grew, and by the end they were, in unison, saying that this was not as hard as they had imagined for years. Without knowing about the other, two of my team members came to me at night to ask, "How can I take this back home with me and share the gospel there?" As I sat with the first, he realized that in coaching his son's little league team, he had a wide-open opportunity to share the gospel with those families. By the end of the conversation, he was planning how he could make time to be with each family to build a bridge of friendship. The second team member did not see how he could possibly adjust the flow of his life to intersect with more lost people until I reminded him that as a newly retired marriage and family therapist, he had a skill that is unfortunately much in demand. He also became so excited as he dreamed about going back home and starting a small group of couples from his neighborhood who wanted to enrich their marriages. This would be the bridge across his street.

And that is what this bricklaying looks like. It would be futile to try and list all the ways that bricks can be laid, but really it usually begins with simple gestures. It means looking and listening for moments in a person's life in which he or she is open. It's listening and looking for a way to bless. Some additional examples may help at this point.

Prayer Bricks

Prayer bricks come in countless sizes and colors, but the reason these bricks are particularly well-suited to bridge building is that it is quite rare, even in our post-Christian culture, for a person to forbid you to pray for them. Now, that doesn't mean they will always be comfortable with you praying over them at that moment but almost without exception people have given me permission to remember them later in my prayer time.

I remember Maria, the waitress who waited on my men's leadership group every Tuesday morning for breakfast. I shared with her one morning that we were about to pray over our food and asked if there was something I could mention to God on her behalf as we prayed. She immediately shared her concern for her son, and we agreed as a group to lift him up in prayer. After a few weeks of praying for her son, I had the opportunity to share the gospel with her one day, and she prayed to trust Jesus as Savior.

There is no limit to how creative a person can be in building these relational bridges. Sometimes they are overt and organized, such as the bridge a friend built at work. He began in his office with simply praying for people anytime they mentioned a need. Later, when a genuine interest in prayer developed, he began a prayer group. When this group came together to share concerns openly, it was natural to share the gospel in this setting. Several of his coworkers trusted Christ as Savior, and the group stayed together for Bible study and even began to do mission projects together.

Another equally effective way to use prayer in an office setting is to simply become an intercessor for people in your office. There does not have to be an organized prayer meeting. Simply keeping a personal prayer journal with a section for your office can help you build a bridge of love to those who desperately need hope.

I was teaching a session on this kind of bridge building a few years ago when a lady stayed behind to ask for more details on how to get started. I told her that if it were me I would go and purchase a nice leather-bound journal and place it on the corner of my desk. I would then listen carefully for any concerns from coworkers. Then as a need was revealed, I would ask that person if I could pray for him or her. I would also let that person know that I would write the request down in my prayer book so I could remember to pray for it faithfully. And the only thing I would ask is that he or she keep me informed about the situation. She decided that she would give it a try. She purchased the journal and began to record the prayer requests of coworkers, being careful to go over them weekly and ask about progress. Sometime later she reported that people grew quite accustomed to bringing requests to her because they knew they would be prayed for faithfully. On one occasion a coworker asked her, "Am I in your book?"

It's gratifying to see the people you are praying for take baby steps toward God as you show a sincere interest in the situations of life. As the Lord works in their lives, they develop trust in Him, and you will find an open door to lead them to the saving kind of trust. Be sure you take that step of sharing the gospel with them early on or you run the risk of inadvertently reinforcing the idea that God is someone you go to only when things go wrong.

Another circle of influence where God has truly blessed bridges of prayer is in neighborhoods. Within just a few months of becoming intercessors in our own neighborhood, we had the privilege of praying for a variety of needs, including the following:

- an impending divorce
- a blood disorder
- a person whose mother was diagnosed with cancer
- a neighbor who lost both mother and father within a few months of each other

- a neighbor who suddenly became the main caregiver of her father-in-law
- a neighbor who is separated from her husband
- a neighbor who had a partial leg amputation due to severe diabetes
- a neighbor who underwent a sudden job change
- and a neighbor who had to place her teenage daughter in a mental facility.

A moving moment occurred when my Jewish neighbor (whom I referred to in an earlier chapter) lost his father suddenly. Although he is a practicing Jew who attends synagogue, he reached out to me when his father died. He called me over to his home just across the street and welcomed me into a family gathering. At one point he physically put his head on my shoulder in grief. It was my pleasure to pray for him during this difficult time, and it led to me being able to share the gospel with him again. In considering this situation later, I realized that there were many bricks that had been laid before this occurred—small bricks like diagnosing car problems, making small adjustments on his daughter's bike, my wife providing counsel regarding their lawn, and my boys loading and unloading heavy objects for them; each of these was a stone in a pathway to sharing the gospel with my neighbor. And although he still has not placed his trust in Jesus, I was pleasantly surprised when he came to an outdoor family event at our church and upon meeting our pastor pronounced that I was one of his best friends!

Sometimes getting started is the hardest part. One idea that worked well for us was to introduce ourselves to the neighborhood while we were still relatively new. A great time to do this is Christmas when it's natural to send out cards. You can create a family Christmas card to put on the doors of your neighbors with home-baked cookies. A colorful, fun card with your family Christmas picture and some information on each family member (including pets) is great. Then, without being preachy, you can briefly mention that you enjoy praying for any needs that may come up in their family. Include your email address, and let them know that these requests will be kept confidential. Then sit back and wait for email prayer requests. You will be amazed. The added benefit of this strategy is that you often get enthusiastic emails from other believers in your area who either attend a different church than you or do not yet have a church home. You may find people who will join you in reaching your neighborhood through home groups or events.

Project Bricks

Another avenue for connecting with our neighbors has been home improvement. With the explosion of do-it-yourself cable tv shows, home improvement projects have become for many a hot topic. Discussing these projects can be a great way to interact. My wife and I are do-it-yourselfers. We have joked that if we got married again, we would only register at Home Depot. In fact, when we had three teenage boys living at home, some of our best dates consisted of a quick bite to eat and an evening of browsing through the home improvement center. We have found that people not only love hearing about our small projects, but they also love to talk about their own.

On one occasion my wife had tired of the carpet in one room of our house and simply ripped it out on a whim and stained the concrete floor underneath. It turned out to be beautiful and has been the subject of several tours for people who are trying to get the courage to do the same. If you are ready to bond with a neighbor, offer to help them do a similar project at their home just for the fun of helping them. By the end of such a project, you will have made significant progress on a relational bridge.

Welcome Wagon Bricks

Still another strategy that can be a wonderful starting point to reaching your neighborhood is to create your own welcome ministry. This one has the added fun of involving your children in preparing some simple gift bags that are then delivered to new families in your area. Some items that can be included are: a simple card of your favorite vendors that serve the neighborhood (local pizza delivery, Chinese takeout, closest urgent care facility, poison control phone numbers, and of course something about your church), some cookies baked by your family, and again, a brief note from your family that has a color photo and your email address stating that you would be happy to pray for any needs that might arise as they get settled.

Some families drop the gift by when the family is home so they can put a name and a face together; still others opt for the much-less-direct approach of hanging the bag on the door without a face-to-face meeting. But whether you check your homeowners' association newsletter for new people or simply keep your eyes out for moving trucks and houses that are sold in your neighborhood, it's an intentional, fun way to reach out where you live.

Event Bricks

The last approach I will mention in neighborhood bridge building is event bridge building. There are several times of the year that provide a natural opportunity to meet your neighbors. Your homeowners' association may even have activities planned at these times. If not, schedule them yourself. Here are some ideas that people have found very successful for event bridge building:

- Block Party—at your clubhouse, pool, or nearby park or stretching across several neighbors' front yards. This one works great at Easter if your neighborhood does not already have an Easter egg hunt.
- Fourth of July Picnics
- National Night Out—a national community involvement event (see www.nationalnightout.org)
- Halloween Night—Encourage two or three families to gather in lawn chairs on a designated front lawn to give out candy together.
- Christmas Cookie Bake-Off and Decorating—Ask several church families to attend as guest carolers.

Combining some seasonal family activities with bridge

building can help keep your schedule from being overcrowded and can model the importance of being a godly influence in your community to your own children.

Regardless of what form ministry to your neighbors takes, the key is to adjust your mind-set and then your schedule. Deciding that interacting with them is more important than finishing your to-do list around your house is no small adjustment. It's important to keep in mind that your neighbors also have a "honey do" list, so you don't want to monopolize their time. Mostly, we just need to go out of our way to speak to them, to ask about their kids' sports, or to compliment them on their yard. Then, if you will generally keep it brief and keep moving, eventually you will find a time when they really want to talk. That's when the sacrifice of time comes because it could be when dusk is approaching and your lawn is half mowed. You may not win yard of the month, but you may be successful in establishing a relational connection that could open a door for the gospel.

Matthew 22 records the occasion where Jesus was asked which commandment was the greatest. Even though the question was a ploy to trick Jesus into saying something for which He could be discredited, Jesus answered the question very directly, and He went on to name the second greatest commandment as well when He said:

"You shall love the Lord your God with all your heart, and with all your soul, and with all your mind. This is the great and foremost commandment. The second is like it, you shall love your neighbor as yourself." (Matthew 22:37–39 NIV)

It is a powerful thought that, next to loving God, loving my neighbors is the great desire of God's heart. We are not promised overnight results or any results for that matter. But it is clear that followers of Jesus have retreated largely to our Christian bubble while the world marches headlong into an eternity without Jesus. Surely it's time to take some simple, practical steps to show the love of Jesus to those with whom we live.

CHAPTER 9

Let's Talk Tools

I love tools. When I was growing up in Corpus Christi, Texas, I loved going with my dad to shop for tools at Sears. My dad owns an amazing collection of tools, including multiples of every one. So, because my dad loved tools, we went to Sears a lot. I loved it because they served fresh popcorn! Still today, when I enter a store that serves freshly popped popcorn, it takes me back to those Saturday mornings. I have inherited my dad's love for tools, and I now own quite a collection of my own. Included in this collection are tools for welding, bending, cleaning, grooving, grinding, cutting, filing, and more. And I'm still accumulating them today. Take me to a good tool store and time seems to stand still.

I remember my mom and dad having discussions before we would leave for a trip to the tool store. She would tell him not to buy the store out. And he would remind her of the maxim he lived by: "You gotta have the right tools to do the job right."

That's true when it comes to sharing the gospel as well. The right tool can make a huge difference. Another thing my dad says about tools is that every time you use one, you become more proficient in its use.

Finding a good tool to use in personal evangelism is important because an ineffective tool is one you won't pick up very often because it just doesn't fit. On the other hand, when you find one that's effective and suits you well, you will go to it often.

As I have served in various capacities in churches the last few decades, I have been so blessed to learn various ways to share the gospel, and each has left an impression on me. In fact, parts of each of them are embedded in my heart and are like arrows in a quiver I call upon depending on the situation at hand. However, every archer or bow hunter has his favorite arrow, and I have come to love one in particular for sharing the gospel. As we have discovered and developed this tool over the last few years, we have come to call it the Helping Hand to Christ.

When I accepted the role of missions and evangelism pastor of a church in 2005, I asked the Lord to show me an effective gospel presentation that I could pass on to people who were interested in learning how to share the gospel. Although it had been many years, God brought to mind a simple graphic that uses the fingers on your hand to illustrate the truths of the gospel. As with so many things in life, its beauty lies in its simplicity. The Lord allowed me to revise it into something that is unique and powerful. In the last ten years, God has used this tool to equip over three hundred people to be effective witnesses in most any situation. The stories that come back from those who are discipled in this area are gratifying. Moms and dads are now leading their children to Christ instead of taking them to one of their pastors. People are sharing the gospel at work, and it has even proven to be effective overseas in China, Uganda, and Zambia. Allow me to share with you why I believe it has been so effective.

First of all, as I stated earlier, it is simple. The older I get, the more I understand that whether you are talking about home decor or word economy, less is more. This is a strength of the Helping Hand to Christ. It is not a long, complex presentation. It is simple to memorize, simple to share, and simple for a person who has not yet received Christ to understand. It is not necessary for people to grasp a lot of deep theological concepts to trust Jesus. I doubt very seriously if the jailor written about in Acts 16 would have been better served by a theological treatise than by the simple words, "Believe on the Lord Jesus Christ and you will be saved."

The second reason I love this method is mnemonics. A mnemonic device is simply a memory device. Like remembering a list of items by making up an acrostic, these devices rely on associations between something that is easy to remember and something that is harder to remember. In using the Helping Hand, your hand becomes a visual in which you associate each finger on your hand with an important spiritual concept. As I have taught this to people over the last few years, they have come back to tell me that because each finger visually represents the truth they are to share, they are able to move through the steps of sharing Jesus easily. Because they are not grasping for each point, they are free instead to focus on the person they are talking to and to listening to the Holy Spirit as well.

The next reason it is so effective is that it's fun! That's right; it's fun. It is fun to learn, it is fun to share, and above all, it is fun to hear. I cannot tell you how many times I have asked a person for permission to share some spiritual truths using the fingers on my hand, and they get this look of curiosity that causes their defenses to immediately go down. Likewise, there have been so many times that, as I develop the idea and they begin to get the memory associations, they smile right in the middle of the conversation and even comment, "I like that." And this has proven to be equally true regardless of age.

I also like the fact that it is convenient. As hard as I try to make it a constant in my life, there are still days when I find myself without a tract. There are times when I have met with people and grabbed a pencil and a napkin and drawn an illustration to share Christ. Then there are many times when I have no pencil, not even a napkin; however, I pretty much always have my hand with me. I guess you could say it's handy!

Finally, I love the Helping Hand to Christ because God is using it! As a pastor, my heart's desire has always been to see God raise up an army of well-equipped warriors from within our church who would do more than rattle the gates of hell but storm them and do what Jude 23 says, "Save others by snatching them from the fire" (NIV). We began by taking two men and modeling this tool with them for about three months. They caught the passion and trained two more. Within just a few cycles of this training, we had eighteen teams totaling fifty-four people who were gathering to learn about evangelism.

We added an on-the-job-training component, which proved to be an integral part of our process because teaching the biblical principles of evangelism without taking people into real-life situations to share the gospel produces what I call spiritual fatheads. A spiritual fathead is a person with a head full of knowledge that is never applied. In the past ten years, over one hundred people have come to trust Jesus through this class. I am so thankful to God for these souls. However, we have always made it clear that these training sessions are boot camp, not our actual deployment. The deployment happens day by day as we, the army of God, are deployed in the avenues of life where people desperately need to hear the good news.

As I speak with pastors around the country, there is a groundswell of sentiment that we must get back to sharing the gospel. After all, the great commission was the last great assignment we were given by Jesus before His ascension. While I hear and read of this groundswell, it seems there are fewer and fewer churches that actually have a consistent way of training their people in a simple, effective tool. That is why you are holding this book. It is my attempt to inspire and motivate people to action, and it contains the best tool I have ever used to share the gospel, the Helping Hand to Christ.

It's been exciting to hear the stories of those who have learned to share their faith in the ebb and flow of daily life. During one class, a widow who had just learned to share the gospel shared her story. She had recently lost her husband to a sudden heart attack. Shortly after this she went on a trip to Jamaica—a trip she and her husband had planned to take together. Through tears of joy she shared how the Lord used her to lead five women to Christ on the island during her vacation turned mission trip. She so loved sharing the gospel that she went on a short-term mission trip to Africa and shared the Helping Hand to Christ there. Finally, she came home and sold all her possessions and moved to Africa to share Jesus with children in schools.

One of our senior adult men shared how, after years of silence regarding eternity, he stood before his entire family at a family reunion meal and used what he learned in our class to share the gospel. A nephew immediately ran out of the room, deeply moved, and later he had the privilege of leading him to Christ.

One of the young men I discipled for over a year became quite burdened about being a witness at work. He works at a scientific research lab and finds himself surrounded by very intelligent people who are skeptical about God. He learned the Helping Hand to Christ and began to talk to coworkers and neighbors. There was one particular man for whom he had a deep burden. The man had retired from the lab, but they maintained their friendship. He was an expert welder, and on several occasions, he had planned to meet the man to be mentored by him. However, on each occasion the man had cancelled due to either illness or depression. My friend felt that he was slipping away into an isolated, depressed state. He had planned to use the welding experience to build a bridge to share Jesus with this man. Suddenly, the man had a stroke and was placed in the intensive care unit. I accompanied him to the hospital, but we were warned by his son that his dad had not been conscious for some time. We were so surprised to find him awake and alert! He could not communicate well because of a breathing tube but his eyes were opened, and he clearly recognized my friend. We shared the gospel with this man together, and even with the ventilator, he whispered a prayer of salvation. It was a moment I will never forget—a moment that only came about because a young man became burdened and got trained to share Christ. The son was surprised to hear that his dad was awake and alert. He slipped back into the coma later that day and within a couple of days was gone.

This simple little tool has revolutionized not only the people's lives who have trusted Jesus through it but the lives of those who continue to share it and have been released to fulfill the purpose for which they were created. It is my prayer that it will empower you to be on mission as well. What follows is a word-for-word presentation of the Helping Hand to Christ. Although there are an infinite number of transitions to get into the gospel, this version includes one transition approach that can be used when talking with any friend or family member.

The Helping Hand to Christ Gospel Presentation

You know, lately I've been reading and studying what the Bible says about life after death, and what I was somewhat surprised to learn is that The Bible says there is a way we can know with 100% accuracy that we have eternal life.

The Bible says it this way: "These things were written ... that you may know you have eternal life" (1 John 5:13 NIV).

Another thing I've learned is that it's not about a person's religion. It's about a relationship with God.

In fact, someone asked me two questions that really helped

me think about my relationship to God. Do you mind if I ask you these two questions?

The first question is: "If something happened to you today, how sure are you that you would go to heaven? Would you say you are fifty percent or one hundred percent or some other percentage?"

The second question is a little different: "If we were standing at the door to heaven and God asked: 'Why should I let you into heaven?' What do you think you would say?"

(Allow time for a response and look for whether the answer is a works response or faith in Jesus.)

If you have a couple of minutes, can I tell you what the Bible says about those two questions?

There are five truths that a person must accept to be certain of his or her relationship with God.

As I explain these five truths, I would like to use an illustration that I think will help you remember each one.

I'm going to relate each one of these truths to one of my fingers.

Let's walk through it together.

First of all is the thumb. In our culture, a thumbs-up is a symbol of something good. Thumbs-down, on the other hand, means something is not so good.

The thumb represents the first truth, which is *good news.*

The good news is that God loves you and wants to be with you now and forever. You see, God did not make heaven just to be a home for Him and the angels. He made it to be your eternal home as well. Not only does God want to spend eternity with you in heaven, but He wants to be with you now as well. He wants to live in you and give you a life of meaning and purpose.

Jesus said, "I have come that they may have life, and that they may have it more abundantly" (John 10:10 NIV).

Next we come to the pointer finger. Where the thumb stands for good news, this finger stands for bad news. When I was a small child, my mom would say, "It is bad to point out someone's faults because when you point at them, there are three fingers pointing back at you."

The pointer finger represents *bad news*. The bad news is that you and I have both failed to live up to God's standards; this is called sin.

Because God is perfect and can't be united with sin then we can't be with Him because we are sinful. A wall of separation has been placed between us and God.

(Use your other hand to form a wedge between your thumb and forefinger to illustrate.)

The Bible says, "All have sinned and fallen short of God's glory" (Romans 3:23 NIV).

But God made a way for that wall to be removed so we could be with Him.

The next finger is our center finger. If you draw a line from the top of this finger down you will see it marks the center of your hand.

It reminds us of the *central message* of the entire Bible, which can be summed up in one statement: Jesus died on the cross to take our punishment to remove the wall of sin and give us the gift of eternal life.

The Bible says, "But God demonstrates his own love toward us in that while we were still sinners, Christ died for us" (Romans 5:8 NIV).

Jesus was God who came to earth in the form of a man. He lived a sinless life and died on the cross to pay for our sins. He was buried and on the third day and rose from the dead, proving He has the power to forgive our sins.

At this point, many people ask a really good question: "If Jesus died for the sins of the world, does that mean that everyone in the world will go to heaven?"

The answer is no.

Jesus died because all sin must be punished. Either we will take the punishment ourselves for our sin, or we will allow Him to take the punishment for us.

By His death He purchased the gift of eternal life for each of us. That gift is offered to you today. However, a gift is not really a gift until it is received.

And that is what each of us must do—we must reach out and receive the gift of eternal life.

Imagine that I went and cleaned out my bank account and cashed in my retirement fund and took it all and bought you an expensive car. I then placed the keys at the front desk of the dealership in an envelope with your name on it with instructions to give you the car. Now, if you refuse to go to pick it up, you would receive no benefit from all that I spent for you.

In the same way, Jesus spent His own blood to purchase the gift of eternal life, but although He has done all that is necessary for you to have this gift, you will not get any benefit from it unless you receive it.

But how does a person receive this gift?

That brings us to the next truth.

The next finger is the ring finger. The left ring finger is where someone who is married usually wears their wedding ring.

That ring is a symbol of a unique relationship of commitment and trust.

God desires to have a unique relationship with us. He wants us to place our trust in Him alone for eternal life.

And just like in many wedding vows the bride and groom say, "Forsaking all others," we must turn our back on our sin and any other way we might try to reach God.

When we sincerely pray and say to God, *"I do* put my trust in You alone for my eternal life," immediately His sacrifice becomes the payment for our sin; the wall of sin is taken away, and we are united with Him.

That leaves just one truth represented by the little finger.

The little finger reminds us of this truth: We must take the *small step* of faith toward God to fully trust Him for eternal life.

We do not need to go and try to clean up our lives first. Only He can truly cleanse the heart.

We don't need to go and try to learn more about the Bible first. Only He can reveal spiritual truth.

That small step is to sincerely pray, placing your trust in Jesus alone for eternal life.

Does that make sense?

If that makes sense to you and you are ready to receive the gift of eternal life, I can help you pray this prayer of faith in much the same way that someone helped me.

As you talk to God, repeat these words after me, but remember, you are not talking to me; you are talking with God.

Dear God, I know You love me and want to be with me now and forever. I know I have sinned and my sin has separated me from You. I believe You died to take my punishment and forgive my sin. I turn away from my sin and place my trust in You alone for my eternal life. I invite You into my life to be my Savior. Thank You, Jesus, for coming into my life and giving me this wonderful gift. In Jesus's name, amen.

Congratulations! You are now a part of God's forever family.

The last part of the hand we see is the palm. This reminds us that in the Bible, God says,

"And I give them eternal life, and they shall never perish; neither shall anyone snatch them out of My hand" (John 10:28 NIV).

You never have to worry about losing this gift of eternal life because our all-powerful God is holding you in the palm of His hand and will never let you go.

Your decision to follow Jesus Christ and to place your trust in Him to be your Lord and Savior is the most important decision of your life, but it is not the end. It is just the beginning of a lifelong adventure of living life with Jesus Christ personally.

When people trust Christ, we then walk with them through their next steps with Jesus by giving them the tract "The Helping Hand to Christ." This tract has been developed to affirm their decision and give them some important direction for spiritual growth.

"The Helping Hand to Christ" tract and additional training resources are available by email request at freeamigos@sbcglobal.net

CHAPTER 10

An Eternal Legacy

It was a Wednesday afternoon during the beginning of the first Gulf War. I was a student pastor at the time in Spring, Texas, when a young man, one of my middle school students, came to me and wanted to talk. I was getting ready for our evening service and had a lot to do, but he looked distressed, so we stopped and talked. He was pretty shaken by the situation overseas, and as we sat and talked, I shared the gospel with him. The Holy Spirit had convinced him of his need for Jesus, and he prayed to receive eternal life that day. I had no idea in that moment what would transpire in this boy's life in the years to come. He grew to be the premier leader in that student ministry and answered God's call on his life to be in ministry. I began to mentor this young man and taught him how to share the gospel. After college, he enrolled in seminary and came to work with me as my assistant. While serving in this capacity, this young man led my son to Christ at the same age I had led him to Christ. I wondered later, what if I had been too busy to sit with him so many years earlier? What if I had sat with him and simply comforted him but had not shared the gospel? What if I had not been trained? And what if I had not trained him to share the gospel? Would my son's salvation have been hanging in the balance? I know God would have continued to pursue my son, but I would have missed out on one of the greatest blessings of my life. I would have missed out on being a part of my own son's salvation story. For God to write this wonderful story of salvation, it was not only important that I lead this young man to Christ, but that I discipled him in how to lead others to Christ as well.

Many years ago, I started writing down the names of those I had the privilege of mentoring in evangelism. It's so rewarding to think back to a few of them. There was Chandra who was already a fired-up believer, who went on to train many others and eventually became an accomplished author who has traveled the world sharing Jesus with thousands in conferences.

There was Jeremy, who went on to become a foreign missionary in Europe sharing Jesus in a land that has virtually forgotten God. There was Zack, a young man who is now a pastor. I had the privilege of traveling to his church to teach his people how to get started actively sharing their faith. And there were Tanya and Calvin. This young couple are now sharing Jesus in a foreign country whose government is hostile to evangelism. There are many more names written in my Bible. The point is that when we started training, I could not see the end. It was just one person or two at a time learning to share their faith. And that's all we're responsible for, pouring into the person God puts in front of us. Do that and the rest will come.

After every evangelism training semester, we have a graduation dinner. I always close that dinner with the following quote.

Anyone with reasonable intelligence can stand under an apple tree and count the number of apples growing on that particular tree. But only God can count the number of trees in an apple. Inside every apple there are seeds that have the potential to grow another tree that has apples that have seeds that can grow additional trees as well. And this cycle goes on and on with results that are humanly incalculable.

That's what happens when we refuse any longer to be timid Christians. This amazing sowing and reaping cycle begins when we wade out of the pool of mediocrity and begin sharing our faith. Slowly and methodically God builds an eternal legacy from one surrendered life. And although you may never know when the man you led to Christ leads someone else to saving faith, you still had a part in the Holy Spirit's sowing and reaping. Jesus promised in John 15 that as we abide in Him, He would produce fruit through us and "fruit that remains." The most powerful and lasting legacy you can leave behind is a trail of people God has impacted through your faithful witness to His love and mercy.

I hope you are ready. I hope this book has motivated and empowered you to begin the most exciting adventure of your life—the adventure of sharing Jesus. Take the time to learn the model presentation in the previous chapter. In fact, I would advise you to learn it word for word at first. I realize that there are people who are critics of using a model presentation to share the gospel. They say that Jesus never shared the gospel the same way twice. And my answer to them is, "You're not Jesus." I don't mean that in an unkind way. But even if you've been sharing the gospel for years, when you learn a new tool, it's best to learn it verbatim at first, and then as you get comfortable with it, you can make it your own by changing the illustrations and phrasing to fit your personality and style.

For some, the idea of pointing out each truth of the gospel using a visual is awkward. It just doesn't work for them. In that case, they simply use it as a memory device internally, to keep them on track, and don't allude to it verbally. It will still help you move from truth to truth in a fluid way that is easy for people to understand.

You are about to embark on the greatest adventure of your life—the evangel adventure. As you dedicate yourself to learning how to share your faith, you can be assured that you will not be one of the 95 percent that stands before God having never told a single person how they can receive the amazing gift of eternal life in Jesus.

Godspeed on your mission.

Printed in the United States
By Bookmasters